TEETERING ON A TIGHTROPE

My Bipolar Journey

Steven W. Wilson

Fulton Books
Meadville, PA

Published by Fulton Books 2022

This work contains graphic material and
may "trigger" certain individuals.

Many of the character's names have been changed.

ISBN 979-8-88505-910-7 (paperback)
ISBN 979-8-88505-911-4 (digital)

Printed in the United States of America

ACKNOWLEDGEMENT

Thanks to the following for their tremendous help in making *Teetering on a Tightrope: My Bipolar Journey,* a reality:

Ashten Evans, editor at Reedsy for her terrific editing and fantastic advice.

Wendy and Matthew Lesko for helping me understand the process and their excellent feedback on the book.

Dr. Robert Gaffey, psychologist, for instructing me on what to avoid writing so I wouldn't get in trouble.

Dr. Amy Bjorkman, psychologist, who gave me the inspiration to write the book.

Jason Fredericks, Fulton Books, who guided me through the publishing process.

Martyn Beeny and David Carriere, Reedsy, for showing me how to implement the plan.

Zane Cole and Marvin Mahoney, Lincoln Creative Writers, for their outstanding work on marketing "Teetering."

CHAPTER 1

The Horror of It

When I was a fun-loving kid of nine, I never dreamed I would face the most terrifying day of my life in a matter of months. One of my first childhood memories from this time was when my best friend, Stocks, and I were rambling along a wooded area near my home, minding our own business, when suddenly we spotted a shed. Venturing into it, we discovered shovels, tools, and gardening supplies. Above our heads was a glass ceiling divided into panes, much like a greenhouse. It was fortuitous for us that one of the panes was missing. We could climb through the opening and slide down the slanted roof into the newly fallen snow.

As an ultrathin, scrawny fifty-pounder, I went first. During my exit, I accidently broke one of the panes, sending shards of glass in all directions. Without further incident, I made it to the roof. My buddy was a heavyset kid and tried to wiggle through the openings but couldn't make it. As he fell to the floor, he spied a hammer. He hoisted himself up to the glass, broke the remaining panes, and scurried onto the roof. We both slid down the roof and then headed toward the woods. Out of nowhere, we heard a loud woman's voice yelling, "Stop! What are you hooligans doing? What are your names?"

At that moment, I had a great idea for how we could escape.

"Tell her you're me, and I'll tell her I'm you. She'll never figure out who we are," I whispered.

So we did and then ran into the woods, howling with laughter all the way home.

The following day at school, the school secretary entered our classroom and told Mrs. Seidel, our teacher, to *send the two Steves to the office*. Knowing we were in trouble, we ambled toward the door.

That's when we saw her—the lady who owned the shed. How could she possibly have found us? She turned out to be a teacher for Delaware City Schools. She was known as a *hard-ass*. I thought she must be psychic, not realizing we had stupidly given her our identities.

Yes, we had been caught, and yes, we were punished. Our parents also had to pay for the broken glass. But honestly, we were just two normal nine-year-olds having fun.

That's how I felt back then: a normal kid having fun. For a time, all was right in my world, until that horrific day at the movie theater.

I loved going to the movies—especially to see Westerns. Every Saturday, I would grab fifty cents from my money jar, jump on my Huffy, and peddle to The Strand, our local movie theater. In those days, we would see a double feature with an intermission in-between. Following the grand closing of the curtain after the first show, I would go to the concession counter to buy popcorn and then saunter over to the old-fashioned Coke machine where the world's greatest elixir would pour into a paper cup that appeared to be hanging in midair.

One Saturday, a stranger quickly put a dime into the machine to purchase the Coke for me. He smiled and asked if I would help him do something in the theater. I thought maybe he needed help cleaning the restroom, as that was my job at summer camp. It never dawned on me that he could not have possibly known that.

At any rate, we entered the restroom and went into a stall. He immediately told me to take down my pants. Frightened and overwhelmed, I did as he asked. Suddenly he grabbed me, performed oral sex on me, and then digital penetration. I tried to resist, but he threw me against the stall wall and started choking me. I struggled to no avail. Then, I slid to the floor. Everything went black. I don't remember exactly how long we were in there, but the next thing I knew he and I exited the bathroom along with someone else I hadn't seen before. As I was leaving, he asked if he could sit with me. Yelling "No!" I hurriedly disappeared into the crowd and never looked back.

"What just happened?" I asked myself. *"Why did he do that to me? What am I going to do? Who should I tell?"*

I decided that no one could ever find out about this. I was still scared, embarrassed, and sure it was terribly wrong to let this happen. How did he pick me? Was it the way I looked? I returned to my seat, acting as if nothing had happened. I would keep that secret for over twenty years.

Not long after that day, I started thinking about killing myself.

CHAPTER 2

The Family

My great grandfather, Clyde Jess Wilson, eloped with his soon-to-be-wife, Clara, in 1894 when he was sixteen. Clyde was five feet and seven inches, average height for that time, and railed thin. He sported a nifty mustache and had prominent ears. They headed to Plain City, Ohio, where he became the first of a line of Wilson haberdashers. He was a bench tailor. In other words, he purchased the fabrics for shirts and clothing he sold to his clients, designed the suits and shirts, and constructed the garments himself. The process for a suit consisting of a jacket and a pair of slacks took approximately fifty hours and sold for a whopping $30. Today, that same suit would sell for over $1,000.

Plain City was a small village about twenty miles west of Columbus. Clyde soon became quite prosperous, and well-to-do men from all over Central Ohio visited his small shop looking for the newest and best in custom clothing.

Clyde and Clara's only child, Leo, was born in 1898. As a boy, he worked at his father's store sweeping up discarded fabrics and threads and making sure everything was in its proper place. He loved the tailoring business and vowed that one day he would make it bigger and better. Leo tended to stand up to boys bigger than him. He never backed away from a fight. Possessing a sharp mind, Leo quickly surpassed the available schooling in Plain City, so Clyde and Clara decided to move to a larger town with superior schools.

In 1911, three years before the start of World War I, Clyde Wilson moved his business to Delaware, Ohio, some ten miles north of Plain City. He opened Wilson's, C. J. of course, on the first floor of the Delaware Hotel. He called the store *C. J.'s* to distinguish it from another men's store in town owned by one Billy Wilson. (Ironically, Billy was found murdered in the basement of his store a couple of years later. The culprit was never found.) C. J.'s became the only men's store in Delaware.

Leo continued working at his father's store until he joined the Army in 1916, during the height of World War I. After his service, he returned to Delaware where he entered Ohio Wesleyan University and majored in business. His freshman roommate was a man by the name of Norman Vincent Peale, soon to be one of America's foremost theologians. His book, *The Power of Positive Thinking*, was a runaway best seller. Leo and Norman remained friends throughout their lives.

From the outset, it was Leo's vision to go into business with his father. The two of them joined into a permanent business relationship right after Leo graduated from Ohio Wesleyan. Business was excellent, so Clyde and Leo moved the business to the larger, vacant First National Bank building. Things progressed smoothly until 1929 when Black Friday hit, and the world tumbled into the Great Depression. During that time, most people had little money for fine clothing purchases, so Leo and Clyde got crafty. After careful planning, Leo devised *The Wilson's Suit Club* which allowed gentlemen to purchase a new suit, which had an average price of about thirty-five dollars, for only one dollar down. The balance was then paid off at one dollar per week, interest free. The plan also included shirts, pants, and other items carried in the store. Essentially, that was how Wilson's, C. J. of course, survived.

During his time at Wesleyan, Leo fell in love with a young, accomplished pianist and vocalist, Helen Burns. Helen hailed from a farm in southwest Pennsylvania that encompassed hundreds of fertile acres. Following Helen's graduation from Ohio Wesleyan, she and Leo married in 1922. In 1925, their only child, my father Tom, was born.

As a child, Tom was extremely skinny and tall with protruding ears, which made him look like a periscope. He was so thin he couldn't pass the weight limit to join the Army. Instead, he became a purser in the Merchant Marines during World War II.

Tom was a very likeable kid who got along with everyone. Everyone that is, except Leo. Leo always demanded excellence with no back talk. Whenever Tom stepped out of line, Leo's punishment was to beat him with his belt. As Tom grew, Leo would lash out at him verbally, continuing this practice even when Tom started working at Wilson's. Tom endured this abuse up until the day Leo and Helen retired to Florida in the seventies. It was clear to me that Leo had little respect for his son.

Tom was in his element in the store. He loved the interaction with his customers, always keeping the conversations alive. He brought the art of selling clothing to new heights. Golf on Wednesday afternoon and Sundays during the fall, spring, and summer was a given. Parties at the country club on Saturday nights was ordained. Scuba diving in Grand Cayman was a must from January through April. Nothing, however, was more important to him than his collection of Revolutionary War rifles, pistols, and artifacts. His collection was nationally revered. All this left little time for his family.

Tom wasn't a violent man. He never hit or yelled at my brother, sister, or me. Instead, he paid little attention to our lives, especially in our formidable years, leaving that chore to his wife, Nancy. Tom and Nancy had met at Ohio Wesleyan when he was a freshman, and she was a junior. Following the war, they married in 1946.

My mother was a petite woman who stood no more than four feet and eleven inches. Having graduated with a degree in music, she was an accomplished pianist, though I rarely heard her play. She was a strict disciplinarian, fond of washing my mouth out with soap if I misbehaved. Once, she walked in on me in the bathroom after I had just peed into one of my sister's toy teacups. As I stood frozen with the cup in my hand, she told me to drink it. After a few scary seconds, I abruptly poured it into the toilet. In one swift movement, she grabbed a bar of soap from the sink and jammed it in my mouth. As she stormed from the room, I noticed she snickered slightly.

Nancy was raised by two aunts who felt she was nothing more than a burden and treated her so. Her father, owner of hundreds of acres of land around Marion, Ohio, was quite successful in the moving and shipping industry. He cherished his daughter but spent little time with her. My mom thought the world of her father, but as she grew older, she became obsessed with the idea that it was her fault her mother had died from complications of childbirth six months after she was born. Without her father to comfort her, she slipped into a depression that would engulf her periodically for several years.

What I remember most about my mother was that she cried and sobbed a lot. Sometimes I heard her screaming at the top of her lungs. I didn't know it, but she had a constant, unrelenting pain in her jaw that became most apparent when we sat down to dinner. To eat, she had to manipulate a small plier-like device between her teeth. This allowed her to open her mouth ever so slightly, permitting her to insert a tiny morsel of food through the space. Night after night, she went through this ritual as my sister, brother, and I watched in horror.

Unable to determine the reason for her pain, she contacted a psychiatrist to see if it was a psychological issue. Following months of one-on-one therapy and electric shock therapy, there was no conclusive answer. She was sent home to deal with it as best she could.

Year after year, she suffered from pain that would appear out of nowhere, last several hours, and then disappear until the next assault. Finally, in 1973, fifteen years after her symptoms began, a renowned brain surgeon at Ohio State University Hospital identified the condition as trigeminal neuralgia, more commonly known as *tic douloureux*. It involves the nerve responsible for providing sensation to the face. Contact between a healthy artery or vein and the trigeminal nerve at the base of the brain can cause excruciating pain.

The doctor explained that while a proposed micro brain surgery would leave her pain-free, there was a possibility that the left side of her face would sag permanently. Without hesitation, she agreed to the surgery. The result was miraculous. The pain completely disappeared, never to come back, and her facial muscles were not affected. Unfortunately, her nasty disposition wasn't changed.

My sister, Sandy, was born in 1946. At eight years old, she was the lead ballerina in the show *Cinderella* for the Humphries Dance

Studio in Delaware. The owner, Ms. Humphries, an accomplished dancer in her own right, hoped Sandy would eventually study dance in New York, but Sandy had other ideas. When she turned fourteen, she had burned out as a dancer, quit working with Humphries, and became a normal high school student. She was blonde and petite just like her mother, but without the emotional baggage.

After graduating from high school, she went to Bowling Green State University in Ohio. Following her freshman year, a prominent physician in Delaware assisted Sandy in getting into the nursing program at Capital University in Columbus. During her first year at Capital, a group of conservative pro-life students from Ohio State gave a talk at Sandy's sorority. She was mesmerized by their discussion of Jesus, a baby's right to life, and the horror of abortion. Right then, she decided to devote her life to Christ and his teachings. When she was shown pictures of discarded fetuses during a nursing school presentation, she was determined to fight to end abortions. As an atheist and a believer in pro-choice, I have constantly been at odds with Sandy on these issues, causing many heated arguments over the years. Sandy was always aware of my mental instability, but I never knew how she fared. On one occasion she lamented, "God has had me suffer during my life, so I might find peace and happiness when I get to heaven." To this day, I continue to be unable to relate to her way of thinking.

Sandy received her nursing degree and became a RN. She spent the next thirty years working at Grady Hospital in Delaware until 1998, when she retired because of back injuries from moving patients. Sandy and her husband, Bill, continued to live in Delaware in the house my parents built in 1950. Their daughter, Jennifer, also lived in Delaware, while their son, Jeff, resided in Lexington, Kentucky.

Tommy, my younger brother, was born six weeks prematurely in 1953. The first four weeks of his life were spent in the hospital as he was a fragile little tyke. Like my father, Tommy's ears stuck out from the sides of his head, which upset my mother so much that she would tape them to the sides of his head, hoping they would lie flat. When that didn't work, my mother gave up in disgust, while Tommy just shrugged, not really caring one way or the other.

He excelled in academics and was a star butterflyer on the swim team. It was a feat that was amazing to watch, as he was much smaller than most of his competition and defeated many of them. After graduating high school in 1971, he enrolled at Wake Forest University in Winston-Salem, North Carolina. Always a skinny, frail boy, he discovered Wake Forest swimmers were much stronger and faster than he was. He didn't make the team.

Scholastically, almost all freshman students at Wake Forest excelled. Tommy found himself lingering in the middle of the pack, which was an unfamiliar position for him. On top of that, he was struggling to find his sexual identity. With all of that crushing him, he felt emotionally overwhelmed and alone. Then he met Joey, and all was good again. Unfortunately, I knew very little about Tommy's time with Joey, but I did know it was quite meaningful and brought Tommy much joy and love when he needed it most.

Tommy graduated college knowing exactly what he wanted to do: work for an airline. In 1976, he began a forty-year career as a flight attendant, instructor, and recruiter for American Airlines. Loving every minute of it, he was paid to travel the world. For several years, he served as the number one flight attendant on flights between the United States and Europe and Asia. French, his second language, came into play on many flights, especially to Paris. He retired in 2021 and now works part-time for Breeze Airlines as a recruiter. He and his partner, Michael, live in Dallas, Texas.

Because Tommy was five years younger than me and we were never in the same school together, we didn't really interact with one another while growing up. In many ways, we didn't know or understand much about each other. That changed late in life when, in 2005, he revealed he was gay. Up until then, I had never been sure of his sexuality. When I told him his sexual preference didn't matter to me and that I hoped he was happy, it paved the way for us to become good friends. From that point on, I was able to tell him about my past mental issues, and he shared that he, too, had been plagued with mental issues for years because Mom never let up, always pushing him from one activity to the next, and never letting him find his own way. When it came to his relationship with our father, he acknowledged he had none. Like me, he felt dad didn't have time for him.

As I reflected on my family's interaction with their children, it is clear to me that mom and dad's negative influence on the three of us led to mental anxiety that plagued us the rest of our lives—particularly mine. If only my father had shown me respect and love, I might have escaped many of my demons.

CHAPTER 3

It Begins

In early spring of my fourth-grade year, my family had just returned from a two-week vacation in Treasure Island, Florida. I had been allowed to go because I was a top student, and my teacher figured it wouldn't be a problem. It was a great vacation. The weather was perfect. The food was wonderful, and being in a hotel was the most fun of all. We ran up and down the corridor, laughing and screaming whenever we could. Time flew by, and all too soon I was back in frigid, snowy Ohio, about to return to school. For some unknown reason, I found myself unable to adjust to being back. I didn't want to participate in class. Doing homework was impossible, and my desire to participate in after-school activities was gone. My typically stellar grades dropped like a rock. My teacher informed my mother at a parent-teacher conference that if I couldn't get my act together, she would suggest I repeat fourth grade. Mom's reaction? She never even bothered to ask me what was going on.

Unaware that this was the first of many episodes of depression I would have throughout my life, I lived in silence. Alone in my room, I took a small piece of paper, wrote myself a note, and then stuffed it into my bedroom desk drawer where it remained for several years.

I didn't realize that depression comes and goes on its own time-table. For a few weeks, it was overwhelming. What engulfed me was a feeling of nothingness. I think I was eventually able to return to my former self because I was considered a good athlete and had several close friends, like Stocks, who helped me through the incident.

When the school year ended, my teacher said to me, "It was a long hard fight, but you made it. Enjoy fifth grade."

I thanked her sheepishly and ran out to play baseball with my buddies, acting as if I was on top of the world. It wasn't until many years later while cleaning out that dusty old desk that I came across that yellowed note I had written that year. It read, "If I fail fourth grade, I will kill myself."

CHAPTER 4

Football

For the next two years, I felt like a normal kid. There were no instances of depression as fifth and sixth grade flew by. My grades were great, and I had a ball playing flag football and basketball with my buddies. Suddenly I found myself in junior high school. Having been a speedy running back on our flag football team, I decided to try out for the seventh-grade team. I hated it. The constant working out and running was bad enough, but the hitting and tackling was frightening. Then there were the showers. Thirty naked, sweaty guys crammed under too few showerheads was too much. One kid who considered himself a *tough guy* had an erection. Out of nowhere, images of the bathroom at the theater appeared in my mind. It was overwhelming. I had to escape.

Every day, I went to practice but never put on my shoulder pads. Instead, I went over to the field where the high school team played and watched them until my own team had finished for the day. Then I headed home, acting as if it was just another typical day. That ploy went on until the season was over. I don't know how I got away with it, but no one ever asked why I didn't participate. My parents never found out about my deception. All I knew was that if I had continued playing football I would have spiraled out of control.

Seventh grade rolled into eighth, and I didn't go out for football. Instead, I took up golf. Within a few months, I had steadily improved to where I was consistently shooting in the low eighties. On top of that, my grades soared, resulting in a scholastic ranking of eight out of the eighth-grade class of two hundred ten students at the end of the school year.

My life was back on track until one summer day before I went on to high school. I was enjoying a round of golf when my mother appeared out of nowhere. She informed me that high school football practice was starting the next day and I was going out for the team. I was dumbstruck. Football again? What was I going to do? How was I going to survive that horror a second time? I had no choice. Never had I stood up to my mother before, and I didn't then. So the next day, I went out for the team. It was worse than before. Not only was the hitting and tackling more bone-jarring but there were sixty guys in the shower, and most of them were older and bigger than me. The entire situation overwhelmed and frightened me to the point where I constantly considered injuring myself during practice thinking the pain would numb me from the pressures I was under. But I was too frightened to try.

As the weeks lumbered by, I retreated inwardly. It didn't help that my class schedule consisted of college prep classes filled with the smartest and brightest students in the ninth grade. It seemed as if they knew exactly what they were doing and where they were headed. I felt lost and completely out of place. There was no way I belonged in their world.

Each day was worse than the one before. My grades plummeted. At night, sleep eluded me. I was too tired to pay attention in class. I felt totally inferior to my classmates. Once again, I felt alone and helpless. But my biggest problem was what to do about football. I was about to find out.

One Sunday, I was throwing the football with a friend of mine when I reached for an errant pass. The ball careened off my hand and fell to the ground. At the same time, I felt a sharp pain in the index finger of my right hand. Immediately it swelled up. *Too bad it wasn't broken*, I thought. That would've ended my playing football for the remainder of the year.

Thinking about how close I had come to ending my football career, I retreated to my room. Could this possibly be the answer to my dilemma? Was I brave enough to break my own finger?

In one swift movement, I grabbed my finger and gave it a hard twist. *Crack!* It hung there like a broken branch. The pain was excruciating, but the result was gratifying. Instead of writhing in pain, I was sighing with relief. No more football!

CHAPTER 5

Cheating

With football gone for good, I thought I would return to normal. Instead, I continued to decline. I was a mess. Even the simplest tests at school were impossible to pass, so I added a new element to my arsenal for survival: cheating. It seemed to be the only way I could pass my classes. I became quite proficient at it too. Not only did I get answers by surveying other students' papers but I also wrote answers on paper and stuck them in my sleeves and placed open books in the basket below the chair in front of me. However, on one fateful day in history class, I got all the answers correct by looking at the paper of the student in front of me. The only problem was I had to erase all my previous answers. As soon as my teacher noticed the smudge marks with corrected answers and knowing the girl in front of me was the brightest in the class, she assumed the obvious. The next day in front of the entire class, she accused me of cheating. Proclaiming my innocence, I stormed from the classroom and fled into the hall.

My teacher must have figured that public humiliation was a sufficient punishment. She never brought my treachery up again, but by not having me expelled, she empowered me to continue my devious path throughout the rest of my high school career. I made sure I never got caught again.

If there was a bright spot to my junior year in high school, it was that my golf game was consistently improving. I was scoring in the mid to low seventies, and our team, made up of three other accomplished golfers, was poised to make it to the state of Ohio championship tournament. All we had to do was be one of the top three teams coming out of the district competition.

On the first day of the tournament, I was paired with three novice golfers. Each participant kept score for a different golfer, as we were not permitted to keep our own score. My foursome teed off last. I played well, shooting a seventy-four. As I walked off the eighteenth green, one of my teammates asked me how I had done. When I told him my score, he swore and told me we had finished in fourth place, just one behind the third-place team (but he heard they had cheated). I was terribly dejected.

Upon the completion of our rounds, each foursome went to the scorer's tent where all scores were tabulated and posted. When asked my score, the guy who had kept my card told the person in charge I shot a seventy-two. Now, every golfer knows exactly what they shot, so I knew it was a mistake. I grabbed my card before it was posted and discovered the discrepancy. On the seventeenth hole, he had given me a birdie four rather than a bogey six—two shots better. If I said nothing, that meant we had finished in third place and qualified for State. It would be a huge lie, and I didn't know for sure if the other team had done anything wrong. Without hesitating, I made up my mind. Instead of doing the right thing, I said nothing, picked up my golf bag, walked out of the tent, and went to celebrate with my teammates, unaware that the action I took would haunt me for the rest of my life.

The reality of what I had done overcame me the next day as I prepared to tee off for another eighteen holes of golf. I was no longer aware of what I was doing. It was as if I had never played before. Feeling uncomfortable as I addressed the ball, I had a hard time swinging the club. Usually, I hit my drives around two hundred fifty yards and kept them in play. This time, the ball came off the club like a wounded duck, traveling one hundred fifty yards and landing deep in the woods. Nothing felt right. For the first time while playing golf, it was as if my thoughts were running amuck. My usual confidence was gone, and I had no control of my game. At practice, I couldn't regain my composure. The tournament loomed less than a week away, and I was freaking out.

My play in the state finals was terrible. The first day, I shot a ninety-three followed by an eighty-two the next day. Because of my dismal performance, our team finished in sixteenth place—well, behind the winners. It was my fault. If I had played anywhere near normal, we would have been in the thick of the tournament.

After this, I crashed into that familiar feeling of worthlessness, plus I felt a profound loss. It was the loss of the right to ever play good golf again because I had violated the most sacred rule of the game: count every stroke. The only thing I had left to look forward to was that basketball season would start in a few months. Little did I know that would end in disaster as well.

CHAPTER 6

Basketball

Midway through my senior year, I was kicked off the basketball team. I was poised to be a pivotal member of our team, and basketball was the one thing I enjoyed. I was the sixth man—the first substitution. For the first few games, I played almost three-fourths of each game. We lost them all, but I had played well.

During the practice following our last loss, one of our players stepped on my foot. Immediately it swelled up, and I had to leave the floor. I couldn't practice for a few days. One afternoon, I went to see the doctor to find out if I could start playing again. Once I had the doctor's approval, I went to tell the coach I was okay to play. He whirled around and called out four names, mine included. He told the four of us to meet him in his office. Upon entering the room, he said, "You're all off the team. You screw around too much!"

The four of us, all seniors and White, were shocked. One of the guys was tenacious when it came to rebounding. Another was an excellent ball handler and could shoot better than anyone else on the team, and the other guy was scrappy as hell. Our objections meant nothing because Coach had made up his mind. We were done as members of the high school team.

I was devastated. Nothing meant more to me at that time than basketball. I wasn't the star, but I loved the game. I couldn't believe it had happened. Something else bothered me too. There had been a lot of racial tension throughout Ohio and the entire country at the time, and Delaware was not immune. African Americans were fed up with low-paying jobs, exclusion from the best colleges, and being placed in poorer areas of the towns in which they lived. However, the two main reasons for the uprising were school segregation and voting rights.

My father's store and one restaurant had been targeted for retaliation because of the belief by some that African Americans couldn't frequent those establishments. They were wrong, and, in the end, neither business was bothered. When Coach immediately chose three inexperienced Black kids and a White kid to take our place, I got the feeling Coach had been manipulated into his decision to replace the four of us.

The season continued without us, but the team didn't get better. It got worse, winning only four games. None of the kids who replaced us got much playing time. In my opinion, we had been used as scapegoats to gloss over the challenge of really facing the racial division that engulfed Delaware.

Immediately, I sank back into depression. Basketball was the real joy in my life, and it had been yanked away. Almost all my enjoyment came from playing on the basketball team. It was like a *high* to me, and there was nothing that could replace the feeling I got when I hit a fifteen-foot jumper. Even when I played a great round of golf, I never received the same satisfaction I did from a victorious game of basketball. After that, nothing about being in high school mattered anymore. Instead, I just wanted to get it over with as quickly as possible.

CHAPTER 7

Rollins College

With newly-found time on my hands and the desire to get away, I began investigating colleges to attend. The United States government, in all its infinite wisdom, exempted from military service any male going to college—a great incentive for me as Vietnam was heating up. I had always disliked the gloomy Ohio weather, so I asked my grandparents, who lived in Florida, if they would take me to visit schools in the Sunshine State.

As soon as I saw Rollins College, I knew that was the school for me. Located in Winter Park, the cream-colored buildings with burnt orange-tiled roofs were the epitome of Spanish architecture. Oak and cypress trees were plentiful, and peacocks walked freely among them. Surrounded by Lake Virginia, Rollins offered a myriad of water and land sports, a renowned theater department (Buddy Epson and Tony Perkins were graduates), and independent studies for a student body that numbered one thousand two hundred. There was only one problem: How was I going to be accepted with my less than stellar grades and low SAT scores?

Following my interview at Rollins, I was convinced I would not get in. In February, I received a letter that read, "Welcome to Rollins. See you in the fall." I was in utter shock. I even asked my mother if it was a mistake. She assured me it wasn't. It finally sank in that perhaps my grandfather had given a generous donation to the college. What other explanation could there possibly be? I never found out.

I was looking forward to freshman orientation until I discovered that it was scheduled for the third week in September. That was the same week as our county fair and its Little Brown Jug harness racing classic. This was one of three races that made up the Triple Crown for standard bred pacers, and it was always held in Delaware. With its many events, plus money flowing toward local businesses, the county fair was a big deal for the town. Even the schools were closed for *Jug Day*.

As a distinguished member of Delaware, my father had been elected to the Little Brown Jug Society's Board of Directors and served for many years. Each year, my parents held a cocktail party in their home for national sportswriters, other board members, and local socialites. It was an event not to be missed. Therefore, my folks decided to put me on a plane to freshman orientation by myself rather than make the trip with me. I felt disappointed, nervous, and very much alone.

In preparation for the fall curriculum, all incoming freshmen were required to read two textbooks during the summer. The subjects were humanities and social science. Lacking concentration and interest, I couldn't get past the first few pages of either. Reading and retaining what I had read were impossible. I was unprepared from the beginning.

That trend continued through my first semester. I wound up with a D+ in humanities and an incomplete in social science. My other classes were equally pathetic. I slept most of the time as my depression took hold. Even though I was surrounded by hundreds of fun-loving young people, I felt alone and afraid.

One evening, I met with my social science professor, a plump, bespectacled gentleman in his early sixties. I knew him as a good guy who was willing to work with his students. We talked about my inability to adjust to the rigors of college life. I convinced him it was due to my depression, and I could use a little help. I asked him for a better grade than I deserved. The next day, my incomplete turned into an acceptable B-.

The semester ended without further drama. I returned to Ohio knowing the B- I had received was enough to keep me off academic probation. No one was the wiser.

When I went home for Christmas vacation, my parents were appalled—not at my grades, but at my long hair. The Beatles had bursted onto the music scene in the mid-sixties, sporting long, floppy hairstyles. Shaggy was *in*. I bid goodbye to my short haircut and joined the rest of the world in growing my hair. One of my dad's contemporaries told his son he would disown him if he ever grew his hair like me.

Although I was able to escape getting my hair cut during Christmas break, I did get one when I returned home for the summer. When finished, the barber looked at me and said, "I think your father will be happy."

He had given me a short, childish haircut straight out of the fifties. My father had evidently paid him off to change my look. It took at least three months to get it back to where I liked it. From then on, a friend of mine at school cut it whenever necessary.

When I returned to campus following Christmas break, I encountered one of the most trying events of that year. I pledged X-Club, a local fraternity. Right away, I knew I had made a mistake. I grew not to admire the active members but to fear them as they tried to humiliate the pledges.

My *big brother* was the worst. He was my resident advisor with whom I had cemented a close relationship and had previously respected. That changed when his role as pledge trainer became apparent. At one of our weekly frat meetings, he singled out a pledge who had missed an activity. Forcing the pledge to stand, he took out his paddle and whacked the kid so hard that he landed headfirst into a wall. All the active members laughed and hooted as if it was the funniest thing they had ever witnessed. I had always disliked violence and was horrified.

Then I found out about *Hell Week*. It was the last week before initiation into the fraternity. Basically, it was a week of public humiliation for the pledges. One instance involved a long strand of twine tied to each pledge's genitals. The string was fished up through his shirt and over the collar. A note card that was attached to the end hung snuggly around his neck. When pulled, his genitals would receive a sharp tug. Pledges were dispersed to collect as many signatures on the card as possible from those female students who had pulled the card.

As if that wasn't enough of a disaster, all week-long pledges would take turns crouched on all fours in front of the fraternity house with collars and leashes attached to their necks. It was their job to *bark* at every girl who passed and lift their leg as if urinating on them.

All this childishness infuriated and scared me. Greek life was a major aspect of Rollins. Fraternities socialized with each other, competed in sports, and provided community service to Winter Park. I longed to break ties with the X-Club, but I was afraid I would be ostracized from joining another fraternity. For days, I fretted over what to do until I couldn't take it any longer. Removing my pledge pin from my shirt, I went to our pledge trainer, my previous friend, handed him the pin, and walked away without a word. To my amazement, my decision was endorsed not only by some fellow pledges but also by several guys in other fraternities. I felt more confident and comfortable when I decided to join Lambda Chi Alpha the next fall. I had a lot more friends at Lambda, and they welcomed me with open arms.

CHAPTER 8

Sue, Christy, Megan, Patty, Sherry, and Jennifer

In the spring of my freshman year, I tried out for the men's golf team. Rollins had always had one of the premier teams in their division, so the competition was quite intense. There was a qualifying tournament to see who might be selected to represent Rollins. I had no idea what to expect, as I hadn't played in months. Surprisingly, the first nine holes went well. I shot one over thirty-seven on a course I had never played. I fell apart on the back nine as the old feelings of not being good enough seeped into my consciousness. I shot a disastrous forty-five that knocked me out of the competition. My college golf career ended right then and there.

There was one good thing that came out of the experience—I met Sue, a member of the ladies' team. I did manage to play one round of golf with her before not qualifying for the team. She proved to be one of the best female golfers with whom I had ever played. Almost immediately we hit it off and started dating.

In those days, Rollins had a curfew for all female students. They had to be in their dorms by 10:00 p.m. during the week and by midnight on the weekends. Men, however, could come and go as they pleased. Before the dorm lights flickered off and on to signal it was curfew, we would go to the library or the student union for a couple of hours each night.

One warm southern night with thousands of stars overhead, we took a stroll along Lake Virginia. Along the way, we found a spot on the soft manicured lawn, embraced, and then laid down. I realized something was terribly wrong because I felt nothing—no excitement or anticipation. Nothing, that is, except fear. I couldn't get beyond some kissing and touching Sue's breasts. For some reason, the delusion of a security guard watching us leapt into my head. Looking quite confused and without saying a word, she stood up, brushed off her skirt, and then together we headed back to her dorm. When we reached the front door, I was surprised that she kissed me good night, smiled, and said, "See you tomorrow."

The following Saturday, I borrowed my fraternity brother's car and picked her up to spend the day together. As we drove away, Sue said, "Let's go to a hotel for the day."

I responded that I'd rather go to a movie.

Stunned, she just looked at me as we pulled into the theater's parking lot. She was really pissed off as we got out of the car, and she let me know it. I felt nothing but relief as we headed into the theater. Over the next few weeks, we spent a lot of time together without any further romantic entanglements. The school year ended quietly. I returned to Ohio, and she headed home to North Carolina.

Summer was a stress-free time for me. I was a lifeguard at the Delaware County swimming pool, affectionately known as the DCP. I was paid a whopping one dollar an hour to sit in the guard chair and watch mostly young children have the time of their lives. Each morning, I taught junior and senior lifesaving, and occasionally around midnight, several of us would go frog gigging at local ponds. The object was to shine a bright light into the frog's eyes, causing them to freeze in place. Then we'd take a gig—a long pole with three sharp prongs jutting out from one end—spear the frog, and then place it in a bag. In the wee hours of the morning *Frog*, the DCP's manager (who derived his nickname not from gigging but from his deep, raspy, frog-like voice), would hit the frogs with a shoe, cut off their legs, and then cook them in a French fryer. Ten minutes later, we would enjoy a scrumptious snack that tasted like chicken. Occasionally, we would close the pool, claiming inclement weather, and then head to Scioto Downs, a fancy horse-racing venue in Columbus. We would place our two-dollar bets (more often losing than winning) and gulp down a few beers.

During that first summer, I wrote Sue every week. She would always respond, leading me to believe that everything was all right. The summer flew by, and suddenly, I was back at Rollins. The very first night back there was a party by the lake. Sue was there, looking radiant as ever. I ambled toward her, but to my astonishment, she turned and walked away. Just like that, our relationship was over. Had I lost her because I didn't sleep with her, or had I done something else to offend her? I don't know why, but I never got in touch with her again—not even to ask her the reason for her ending our relationship. This pattern of not receiving answers as to why I was rejected would continue with future romantic involvements, never allowing me to find closure.

My sophomore year at Rollins was uneventful. Somehow, I managed to get decent grades in most of my classes without cheating. I dated only occasionally when there were special parties.

One day, as I was trying to study for an upcoming exam, I received a phone call from Christy, a girl I had known since my first day at Rollins. She invited me to be her date for an overnight cruise on her roommate's luxury boat. It was to be her roommate and her boyfriend and us, and we would be gone the entire weekend. Without hesitation, I told her I couldn't go because I had to study all weekend for an exam. The fear of going through another sexual fiasco unnerved me. The thought of putting myself through that failure would be humiliating. I didn't go and spent the entire weekend studying for the exam. To make matters worse, I received a D on the exam. Soon afterward, the year ended, and I went back to the DCP where I met the first real love of my life.

Megan was from Tuscaloosa, Alabama, visiting her older sister for the summer. A real beauty, she was small—about five feet and one inch—with short brown hair, an infectious smile, and a laugh that was contagious. Immediately we began spending a lot of time together.

Megan's sister lived in an apartment with her husband and their two sons in a neighborhood surrounded by tall trees and lush green lawns. Megan's room was situated in the basement of the townhouse with an outside door leading directly to her room.

Her sister demanded she be home by eleven o'clock each night. We had no desire to be apart that early in the evening, but I would obediently drop her off at the specified hour and then drive away. I would park a block away and then head off to the basement, hidden in the shadows of the mighty oaks. Silently, she would open the door, leaving us alone in our own private world.

One night as we were snuggling in the basement, she whispered into my ear, "Take off your pants."

"No," was my reply.

With a quizzical look, Megan asked me what was wrong. Instead of telling her the truth, I told her I didn't feel comfortable doing it in her sister's house. Reluctantly she agreed, not realizing I was incapable of performing.

A few weeks later, we were in my basement watching *The Tonight Show* with Johnny Carson. Before I knew it, she was all over me, making it clear that this was the time to cement our relationship. I felt trapped with no way out. Suddenly Carson started playing Carnac the Magnificent, one of my favorite characters. I leapt from the couch, turned up the volume, and said, "Have you ever seen Carnac? He's the greatest! Let's watch."

Not believing what just happened, she demanded I take her home. It was a long, silent ride to her sister's place.

The next day, I presented Megan with a single rose and apologized. She accepted and then asked why I had acted that way. I should have explained it to her but couldn't. Letting someone—anyone—know what I had gone through at the theater was impossible. I just sighed and said, "I'm just not ready."

The summer flew by, and suddenly it was time for Megan to return to Alabama and for me to go back to Rollins. Instead of going straight to school, I flew to Birmingham to stay with her for a few days. One day, we went downtown where I ran into a situation I never encountered in Ohio. After eating lunch, I got up to go to the restroom. When I arrived at the door, it said, "Whites Only." Next to the door was a drinking fountain with a sign above it also saying the same thing. Looking around, I saw a sign with an arrow on it that read, "Negro restroom out back." I knew that generally Southerners were highly prejudiced, but this was shocking to me. When I asked Megan what she thought about Negros, she said she agreed with keeping them away from White people. That was the first time she told me she believed in segregation. I was infuriated, but instead of allowing this to turn into a heated argument, I shook my head and said nothing more. Even though we were on different sides of this issue, I was very much in love with Megan, and nothing could change that.

Our relationship was going great. One night at dinner, she asked her mother to slip off her wedding band so she could look at it. She then showed it to me and said she'd love to have one just like it. The next day, I flew to Orlando, yearning to see her again.

My mother had refused to let me take a car to school and disapproved of any trips to Alabama. Undeterred, I bought an old 1962 Chevy Biscayne for $440. Without telling my mother about the car, I made several twelve-hour trips to Alabama, praying the Chevy would make it. It always did, allowing our relationship to continue well into the first semester at school. Deeply in love, I wanted nothing more than to get married and spend the rest of my life with this perfect angel.

Three or four weeks later, I jumped into my car and headed to Alabama for Thanksgiving vacation. As soon as I saw her, I sensed she had changed. Her giddy laugh was replaced by a look of contempt, as if whatever she was mad about was my fault. Time dragged by like molasses dripping off a plate. Panicking, I did the only thing I could think of: I headed to a nearby gas station to purchase condoms from a box hanging on the bathroom wall. Stupidly, I thought the sight of a rubber would prove to her I was finally ready to have sex. I assumed that would make everything right again. To my surprise, she acted repulsed when I brought it out that night. She looked at it, frowned, and said, "Put that thing away!"

The next morning, I prepared to head back to school. Standing at the curb, neither of us brought up what had transpired the previous night. We simply said goodbye, and she turned and walked away.

I dreaded the long ride ahead as I got into my car. I began weeping as if my life had just ended.

Three days later, I received a letter. Megan got right to the point, admitting she had gotten back together with her old boyfriend. With the realization that our relationship was over for good, I sank into a state of total depression. Once again, as before, I didn't attempt to contact her, which made matters worse.

My college friends did everything to help me through the pain. They fixed me up with dates, made sure I didn't just lay in bed all day, and took me to the dog track. Nothing helped. I couldn't sleep or eat, and I cried so much I thought my heart would break. Luckily, final exams weren't until after Christmas vacation, so I didn't have to add that stress to the remaining couple of weeks before going home.

Before I returned to Delaware, I called my mother and told her what had happened. As my plane landed at the Columbus airport, I trudged down the ramp. Upon meeting me, she threw her arms around me and said, "I knew this would happen. She was no good for you."

Under my breath I said, "Fuck you," and headed to baggage claim.

Delaware was a small town, so it didn't take long before everyone knew my girlfriend had dumped me. That week, I got the best advice from the owner of Pizza Villa, our nightly hangout and home away from home. Leaning over the counter, she said quite seriously, "I heard what you've been going through, and I'm really sorry. The best thing you can do is to get laid."

It almost happened.

While home for Christmas break, I reconnected with Patty, a girl from high school. She was a year behind me, blonde, athletically built, and very playful. We made out a few times, but that was all I could do. We'd sit and talk late at night about anything and everything. We were good friends. In fact, she helped lift me out of my deep depression.

One night, we were sitting on a bearskin rug in my basement when we both got a little frisky. The words of Pizza Villa's owner came to mind. I was determined there and then to lose my virginity.

I would overcome my fears no matter what. I was about to remove my pants when the fear struck. I just couldn't go through with it. Red-faced and embarrassed, I told Patty it wasn't her fault. I just wasn't ready.

After driving her home that night, I started asking myself what was holding me back from going *all the way* with a girl. I wanted to have intercourse, but something was still stopping me. Was it really because of that awful day when I was nine? I had been treating it as if it never happened, but now, I questioned whether it could be connected to my inability to have sex.

When I returned to Rollins a few days later, I resumed teaching golf classes, for which I had been hired at the beginning of the school year. In exchange, I received campus parking privileges and free meals. From the first day of teaching classes, I realized I wanted to make a career out of golf. I loved teaching the game I knew so well. Introducing it to novices gave me a great sense of satisfaction. Could I put all that I had done to destroy my love for the game behind me?

One of my students was Sherry from Columbus, Ohio—just down the road from Delaware. She chose golf to complete her physical education requirement. Like most of my beginners, she knew little about the sport other than it was played in the bright Florida sunshine and took little physical stamina. I treated her the same as every other student, encouraging her in hopes she would want to continue playing the game.

One day, I ran into Sherry in downtown Winter Park, said hello, and kept on walking. The next day, we bumped into each other again at the student union. After talking with her for a few minutes, I asked if she would like to go to a party later that night. She accepted my invitation. Little did I know that my life was about to change forever—for both good and bad.

Our first date was terrific. We drank. We danced. We talked, and we laughed. It felt like I had known her forever. From then on, we were together constantly. I was living off campus in an apartment with a fraternity brother who was never home, so every afternoon, Sherry would come over. And we'd spend the afternoon playing cards while getting closer and closer to the inevitable. One Saturday night, we attended a party at a friend's apartment. By 11:00 p.m., the other three couples suggested the two of us should go home early to *get to know each other better.*

We got into my Chevy and drove straight to the apartment where we were completely alone. As we slipped beneath the covers, there was no tension or apprehension. Everything was perfect, and the timing was right. Sherry was the one for whom I had been waiting.

Every day from then on, we found time to be alone. Our afternoon ritual was to play euchre—a Midwestern card game—followed by a rousing romp beneath the sheets. We were in our own world, playing house like a newly married couple.

From the beginning of our relationship, she told me she wanted to be a dental hygienist. She would need to take the required exam at the University of Florida sometime in May. That sounded great to me, because she could get a job wherever we might decide to live.

The day before her exam, we drove to Gainesville and got a room at the Holiday Inn. Sherry left early in the morning for her test, while I stayed in bed without a care in the world. Later that afternoon, we drove back to Rollins. A few weeks later, she received news that she had passed. We were both happy, and, with the school year ending, I never gave it another thought.

The year ended. We went our separate ways in Ohio but only for a day or two as she lived a mere twenty-five miles from me. A week or so later, she drove to Delaware. Unfortunately, my mother was home and for some reason, greeted her with an icy stare and a host of penetrating questions. Sherry had every right to be unnerved. From then on, whenever she drove to my house, she would park in the driveway, honk the horn, and then wait for me to come out. She wanted nothing to do with my mother.

During the previous spring break, I had taken one of my closest fraternity friends, Bill, to Grand Cayman Island to visit my parents, who had a condo there. His father was the senior vice president of Moore McCormack Steamship Lines, and he helped me get a summer job as a junior counselor aboard the SS *Brasil* cruise ship. It sailed from New York to various stops along the east coast of South

America, plus a couple of the Caribbean islands. We were to depart at the end of June and return by the end of July. The night prior to leaving, I met my Sherry at her house for an evening of *fun* as her parents were away. All went exactly as planned, except when we got into bed, she suggested we not use any protection because she thought that would give her an orgasm. She said she had never had one. Who was I to disagree? I thought it might even add extra pleasure for me. Without hesitation, we threw caution to the wind and curled up in her parents' bed.

The following morning, I flew to New York City to prepare for my month-long excursion at sea. After purchasing games and other necessities, Bill and I went to the docks to meet our fellow coworkers. The next day, we set sail for ports of call in Brazil, Uruguay, and Argentina. It was hard to believe that I got paid to have the experience of a lifetime.

Upon arrival at each destination, mail was distributed to the passengers and crew. After a day of adventure in Rio, I returned to my cabin to find a letter wedged under the door. Realizing it was from my Sherry, I eagerly tore it open and began reading. There was something strange about what she wrote. She kept referring to *"we"* did this and *"we"* did that. Naively, I brushed any negative thoughts aside and headed to an evening filled with thirty excited kids speaking and shouting in a variety of languages.

Before I knew it, we were sailing past the Statue of Liberty, marking the end of our journey. When I returned to Delaware two days later, the only thought in my mind was reuniting with my love. As soon as I got home, I called Sherry to set up a time to get together. I heard a tone of reluctance in her voice as she suggested we meet the following Saturday at the Delaware State Park where she would be camping with her family. It was only six miles from my house. Because it was only Wednesday and she didn't want to meet right away, I surmised that something wasn't quite right.

Early Saturday evening, I drove to the park and found her campsite. Sherry, her brother, and her parents were huddled around a campfire. She grabbed a sleeping bag, and together we set off into the woods. Upon finding just the right spot, she spread out the sleeping bag and motioned for me to get in. After holding each other for a few minutes, she told me she would not be returning to Rollins in the fall. Instead, she would be attending dental hygiene school at Ohio State.

"I've given you more than any other boy, but it's over," she said.

What she failed to say (as I later discovered) was that she was going to work with her old boyfriend after graduation. He was going to receive his dental license, and this had evidently been in the works long before I met her. I realized I was simply an unsuspecting diversion—a truth that broke me into a million dark pieces. Once again, a woman had crushed my hopes and dreams. I swore to myself it wouldn't happen again. As usual, I didn't get in touch with her after our breakup, preventing me from getting any kind of closure.

Two weeks later, I returned to Rollins for my senior year and tumbled into a deep depression. The depression was bad enough, but along with it came a new dimension: massive anger. The tiniest thing would set me off. I would grab the nearest object and hurl it into the air, or I would beat on a wall. As for my new roommate, he turned out to be a druggie who painted his room black and covered the window to block out any sunlight. When he and his girlfriend got a dog that howled all-night long, my stress levels went off the rails. Every night, I cursed their existence. Just about everything made me mad as hell.

For the first time, I also began experiencing physical symptoms brought on by my depression. I began to feel as if I had the flu all the time, along with a constant knot in my stomach. Several times I went to the school nurse who always told me she couldn't find anything wrong. Out of nowhere, I found myself crying whenever I thought about my life. I was in a deep black hole with no way out and no one to turn to for help.

Not letting on to anyone what I was experiencing, I became a master at faking it. Everyone knew me as one of the nicest, most care-free people on campus, but they didn't have a clue about my turmoil. Parties and schoolwork were of little interest to me as I wandered aimlessly through each day.

One afternoon, Jennifer, a girl in the junior class at Rollins, came over and sat next to me in the school cafeteria. We struck up a conversation, and the next thing I knew, she had asked me out on a date. At that time, I really didn't know her well. In fact, I didn't know her name right away, but I agreed to see her the following Friday. We had a good time together, so I asked to see her the next weekend. We had another enjoyable evening and soon started seeing each other on a regular basis. From the beginning, I had no desire to take this relationship anywhere. I thought of her only as a friend. I didn't realize she thought differently.

I continued to go out with her on weekends. One day, Jennifer said she wanted to go to the beach, so we packed up her Taurus and headed out. Instead of going to New Smyrna, where most Rollins students hung out, she drove to her hometown of Ormond Beach. Pulling up to this stunning home right on the water, she invited me in to meet her mother, whom she hadn't seen in weeks. We walked up a long set of winding stairs to her mother's bedroom and knocked softly on the door, announcing she had someone special she'd like to introduce. Without a moment's hesitation, Jennifer's mother bellowed, "Go away. I'm busy. Bring him back another time."

Furious and embarrassed, we fled down the stairs, out the door, and into her car. We drove straight back to Rollins. The day was ruined. I had no idea what to say, so we sat in silence as she dropped me off at my apartment and sped away.

Jennifer began showing up unexpectedly and calling me at odd hours. At first, I didn't think anything of it. Then one night as I was getting ready for bed at one o'clock in the morning, I heard a knock at the door. Pissed because it was so late, I threw open the door to find her standing there sobbing. She asked if she could spend the night. Mad as hell, I told her to go home, slammed the door in her face, and sent her off into the night.

Jennifer had done nothing wrong other than be a bit too aggressive (which I saw as an attempt to take advantage of me). The more I thought about it, the more it infuriated me.

"Great," I said to myself. "I shit on her before she could shit on me."

I headed to my room for another sleepless night.

I had no idea what effect the incident had on her, as I never saw her again. For the first time in my life, I didn't care what outcome my actions caused. No one was going to hurt me again. I decided right then to give up on dating, unaware that in a few months I would begin anew.

CHAPTER 9

Lenni

The first time I met Lenni was at a small gathering near campus on Lake Maitland for an afternoon of skiing, swimming, and boating. It was October—just a month after the incident at Ormond Beach. Lenni's sorority sister had brought a small ski boat to college (yeah, I know what you're thinking. Some kids brought Porsches or Corvettes, but she brought a boat.) As chairman of the boat committee, Lenni oversaw scheduling and maintenance. One of the reasons Lenni chose to attend Rollins was because it had a very competitive water ski team, and she intended to join. She had even brought her skis to school.

When it was my turn to ski, I asked if I could borrow her skis. She told me I was too heavy because they had a weight limit of one hundred and twenty-five pounds. That didn't stop me from grabbing them and putting them on. As soon as I yelled, "Hit it!" one of the bindings broke. Embarrassed, I climbed back into the boat, handed the skis to her, apologized, and didn't talk to her for the remainder of the afternoon. I had made a horrible first impression. I was unaware that I would have another chance to make things right.

It wasn't until January that I thought of her again. A friend asked if I had a date for an upcoming basketball game (I didn't). I considered my options and then told him about the bungled ski episode with Lenni and said I would like to see her again. He knew who she was and said he'd see if she was interested in going out with me. The impression I made on her must not have been memorable, as she had to look me up in the Rollins yearbook. To my surprise, she agreed to go.

We attended the men's basketball game where, never one to hide my emotions, I yelled, screamed, and cursed out the refs. Lenni didn't exactly appreciate my enthusiasm and was embarrassed. Convinced I had ruined the evening, I walked her to her sorority house. I took a chance by cradling her face in my hands, giving her a short, soft peck on the lips, and then bid her goodnight. I later discovered that she was quite impressed with that move.

Although we got off to a rough start, I desired to see her again. I invited her to have dinner at my apartment where I would cook a surprise meal for us. Intrigued, she accepted.

I wasn't a good cook, but I did have one specialty: pork chops. I tossed them into the pan and asked Lenni if she liked pork chops. With a smile and a chuckle, she said, "I don't know. I've never tried them."

"Really? Why not?"

"I'm Jewish. I don't eat pork."

All this time I thought she was Italian. She had dark hair, olive skin that tanned easily, and deep brown eyes. I knew very little about Judaism. Delaware, Ohio, was made up mostly of White Anglo-Saxons with a small contingency of African Americans who lived in one carved-out section of town. As far as I knew, there were only three Jewish families in town—one father was a jeweler and the other two-owned clothing stores. They were all successful businessmen yet were treated much differently than the other Chamber of Commerce merchants. Perhaps jealousy or typical stereotyping played a role in the behavior of their fellow businessmen.

I once asked my mother why people felt the way they did about Jewish people.

"They don't believe in Jesus," she said.

I could tell by the way she said it that she didn't care for them, but, as I didn't believe in any religion, I didn't think much of her feeble explanation. At that time, Mom knew about my relationship with Lenni and that she was Jewish. That disturbed me, but I was not about to stop seeing her simply because my mother was bigoted. My father was just as paranoid about Jews, and it became quite clear they were not happy about my relationship with Lenni. And they hadn't even met her.

Back at school, Lenni and I spent quite a bit of time together. Basketball games (I learned to subdue my enthusiasm), movies, dinners out, and even the library made great dates. We became best friends, although I had no intention of becoming too committed. Before long, sex became part of our relationship, drawing us even closer. Even so, I knew if I wasn't careful, I would be thrown away like all the other times.

In mid-May, Lenni's sorority held its annual spring party. It was going to be one of the final events of my Rollins career before graduation. About midway through the evening, I was standing with Lenni, sipping a Blackjack and water when unexpectedly, my ex, Sherry, walked in. She too was in Lenni's sorority and had returned for a visit. She wore an oversized dress that hid her curves and looked totally out of place. I wondered why she looked out of character, and I was eager to talk with her. So I told Lenni I was going to get another drink and then sauntered over to my old girlfriend. As soon as she saw me, she smiled and asked how I was doing. I shrugged and asked if she needed a drink. I surmised she had returned to tell me she had made a huge mistake and wanted me back in her life. At least, that was what I wanted. However, without warning, she whispered, "I can't do this," turned, and hurried away, tearing me apart once again.

Shocked and wounded, I grabbed Lenni (who didn't know what had happened) and whisked her onto the dance floor in hopes of salvaging the evening. For me, however, the damage had been done.

A horrific feeling took over my body and mind. Dread, despair, anxiety, and profound loss completely engulfed me. This was not the usual depression I had suffered for years. It was much deeper. After it surfaced, I couldn't sleep, but all I wanted to do was lay in bed. Diarrhea was my constant enemy, and I lived on Rolaids. Nothing or no one, including Lenni, could raise my spirits. I didn't care if I lived or died. That was the moment true, chronic depression took over my life.

Somehow, I got through the next few weeks. I was doing my student teaching which took a lot of my time. Completing the necessary courses to get my secondary education teacher's certificate was a struggle, but I persevered. I graduated from Rollins in May and then drove Lenni home to Philadelphia before heading to Ohio. There, I met her parents and two brothers for the first time. I could only imagine what they thought of me, as I could no longer mask my depression and felt practically brain-dead the entire visit. In fact, one evening Lenni and I were sitting on the porch when her mother, Tobie, walked in. She quickly turned away and left as her eyes welled up with tears. She obviously didn't think much of me. I wouldn't have either.

There was another reason her mother disliked me: I wasn't Jewish. Lenni's family neighborhood was a blend of Irish Catholics, Protestants, and Jews, and most everyone got along with no problem. I soon realized it was not okay with Tobie if we were more than friends, and I might be a future son-in-law. Lenni's father, Farrel, an avid golfer, warmed up to me when I told him I might make golf a career. I felt her older brother, Dewey, agreed with her mother, while Budd, Lenni's other brother, told me if Lenni liked me, it was all right with him.

CHAPTER 10

Teaching

A week later, I drove home without a clue as to what I was going to do or how to survive under the weight of this oppressive feeling. My family had no way of knowing what I was going through, as I was not very communicative. They had paid a lot of money for me to go to Rollins, and they expected me to know exactly what I wanted to do with my life. Instead, they got a lost, miserable, angry, and unresponsive college graduate.

Instead of trying to find meaningful employment, I went back to lifeguarding. At night, I would hide out in my room, staring into space. I felt nothing. Talking to Lenni every day didn't raise my spirits either. Instead, I got some relief from an unexpected source.

In July, I was asked by the Ohio Wesleyan golf coach to attend a teachers-only golf seminar in Cave Creek, Arizona. I decided to go even though I wasn't up for it. It proved to be challenging and further cemented my desire to make golf a career, but, instead of pursuing the steps necessary to make it a profession, I returned home and continued to sulk, unable to focus on or do anything. I was also plagued by the fear of impending military service. Earlier in the summer, I had undergone the required physical exam in which the doctor discovered I suffered from high blood pressure. For three consecutive days, I was tested to determine if it was bad enough to keep me from serving. It was. I finally received word that I was classified 4F. No military service for me. Now, all I had to do was figure out how to get a job.

One afternoon while at the pool, I received a call from the principal of a middle school in Fort Pierce, Florida. I had interviewed with him in April but heard nothing from him until that day. He offered me a teaching position starting in August. The only thing I knew about the school was that its student population was mostly African American. I accepted his offer. After all, it was a real job, and I would only be two hours from Lenni.

At the end of summer, I loaded up my 1968 Mercury Montego and drove to Philadelphia to spend a few days with Lenni before going to Fort Pierce. Her older brother took us by train to New York City to see the hit Broadway show *Company*. During the second act, my heart began to race, and sweat started running down my back. I wanted to leap out of my seat and tear out of the theater. As calmly as I could, I excused myself and headed for the bathroom. I had no idea what to do. Never had I felt like that before. I was scared to death something physical like a heart attack was happening. Splashing water on my face did no good to relieve the symptoms, so I had an usher summon Lenni. Seeing my distress, she immediately got her brother and hustled me out of the theater, and we headed to the train station. Two hours later, we were back in Philly. Lenni's brother was angry, as he had been looking forward to seeing the play for months, but I ruined the night. It was clear he wanted little more to do with me.

The next day, I caught a flight to Ohio to consult with my family doctor. Following a routine examination, he informed me I had experienced a severe panic attack, which could feel like a heart attack. He assured me it wasn't. He gave me a bottle of pills for anxiety, with instructions to take them as needed. I didn't take the pills as I thought I could get through on my own.

Feeling better, but not understanding the significance of the attack, I flew back to Philly. Two or three days later, I said my farewell to Lenni and started the two-day trip to Fort Pierce. I had very little money, didn't know anyone there except for my grandparents, and had no place to stay. I was in trouble before I even started working.

Soon after arriving in Fort Pierce, I met a guy who was looking for a roommate. He seemed nice enough, so I accepted. He had already rented a furnished house, so it was an easy move. I had to proceed quickly as it was the weekend before first-year teacher orientation.

The orientation went well, but when I returned home, I found my new roommate in his room snuggling in the arms of another man. That was my first encounter with homosexuals, and I worried about being around them. When I was younger, kids would say, "So and so is gay," but it meant nothing to me. All I knew from growing up in Delaware, Ohio, a staunch, conservative town, was that being gay made you an outcast and the butt of derogatory comments. The situation was unnerving. I had to get out of there. Without a word, I packed up and left, never paying my portion of the rent. Once again, I had no place to live.

Fortunately, a close friend of my grandmother's owned an apartment house by the beach. She said I could stay there for $200 per month. One problem: my paycheck came to less than $400 per month. I wondered how I was going to get by, but, since I had no other option, I accepted her offer.

Classes began the following Wednesday. I was hired as an American history teacher, but since I was new, I was given geography classes that were comprised entirely of remedial students. My student teaching had been done at a top-notch school in Orlando with mostly exemplary students. I had no training of how to work with remedial students. Making matters worse, I had never taken a geography course in college. From the start, the prospect of being successful was less than bright.

On the first day of school, one of the students was beaten in the bathroom. The assailant jumped him because the kid refused to give him his lunch money—all thirty-five cents of it. The perpetrator was caught and sent to juvenile detention for six months. A week later, one of my students was raped in the same bathroom, and a teacher had his car stolen. This was not a great start to the year.

Those incidents were not even the biggest problem. It was my depression. It was so deep that I couldn't function. Unable to prepare lesson plans, I went into each class totally unprepared. My seventh and eighth graders quickly sensed my uselessness and took complete control of my classes. Nothing got done, and they had a great time talking out of turn, fighting, walking around, and basically doing whatever the hell they wanted. The noise level was so loud that other teachers began complaining.

"Take control of your class, or I'll find someone who can," barked the vice principal.

All I could do was nod my head, return to my classroom, lower myself into my chair, and feel overwhelmed. It went on like that for six weeks until one day, a horrible display of punishment occurred between one of my students and the vice principal.

A seventh grader had thrown a paper airplane right in front of me. I marched him to the vice principal's office and told him what had occurred. The principal—a huge African American man about six feet and two inches and three hundred pounds—asked the boy if he had thrown the airplane.

"Yes," he softly responded.

"Then you get four swats from my paddle," the principal announced. Reaching into his desk drawer, he produced what looked like a large paintbrush. I could see that it had a wooden handle with a wickedly thick leather brush. He told the boy to stick out his hand, palm up. He wound up like a baseball pitcher and hit the boy's palm so hard that the kid fell to the floor in agony.

"That's one," the principal bellowed. "Three to go."

The vice principal wielded the paddle for a second time, but the kid pulled back his hand just enough that the brush only struck his fingers. Again, the boy wailed as he hit the ground.

"You moved. That one doesn't count," roared the big man.

Slap! Slap! Slap! was the sound that whooshed through the air as the boy was reduced to a ball on the floor. When the punishment was over, I helped the boy to his feet, took him to the restroom, and said, "I'm so sorry. Had I known what he would do, I wouldn't have taken you to him."

With tears streaming down his face, the boy gritted his teeth and grunted, "We're going to get you, *Mister* Wilson."

The next day, I resigned. As I walked away—a beaten and a complete failure of a man—the vice principal frowned and said, "I knew from day one you wouldn't last. You always appeared to be in a daze, like you weren't present. I hope you get your shit together."

"So do I," I muttered.

I needed to get out of town as quickly as possible, so I headed to Winter Park to stay with Lenni for a few days. On the way, I began thinking about my prospects for finding another job. It was obvious to me that I had few opportunities. Who would hire a guy who had lasted just six weeks in his previous job?

What was I going to do? Against my better judgment, I decided to call my father and ask if I could work for him. In truth, that was the last place I wanted to work. I had no desire to become the fourth generation working in the family business.

After my short stay with Lenni, I drove back to Ohio to begin my new position as a clothier. As I looked around my old bedroom, all I could wonder was how I wound up back home. I felt alone and worthless. Just knowing that in the morning I had to go to work for dear, old Dad caused an anxiety attack that lasted well into the night.

CHAPTER 11

On the Road

My father had never been a big part of my life—he was always too busy for the family. I was now going to find out if I had misjudged him. It didn't take long to realize that I had not. There was no written employment contract (after all, he was my father) but rather general points to which we had agreed.

Understandably, I was shocked when he lowered my starting salary to something less than what I had made teaching. As for my duties, I was told I would learn every aspect of the business, but all he had me do was stand around waiting for a customer or straightening the stock. I soon discovered that most customers wanted to work with their favorite salesperson. Basically, I had little to do and was terribly bored—not an ideal situation for someone suffering from depression.

After working in the store for a few months, my father informed me that I was going to work for a traveling salesman by the name of Sam, who sold a suit line to the store. I still couldn't stand up for myself, so I agreed. My salary was even less than what my dad was paying me. Only I seemed concerned about my pay or why I was doing this, but off we went.

Together the salesman and I drove throughout Ohio, Michigan, and Indiana. He was a grumpy, old curmudgeon who hardly ever spoke to me. Sometimes he would disappear for a day visiting one of his love interests. I was left in the showroom looking at the fabrics with nothing to do. On one occasion, he didn't come back for two days.

One day we drove to Marquette, Michigan, to see one of his accounts. As I was preparing to show the line, I was overcome with a familiar feeling. I was starting to have a panic attack. I ran out of the store and tore down the sidewalk. The attack lasted about twenty minutes. When it subsided, I stopped running and realized I had no idea where I was. Fortunately, a stranger gave me directions back to the store. When I returned, the salesman was finishing up. He glared at me, told me to pack up, and load the car. He never did ask why I had disappeared. I assumed he really didn't care. He must have been as sick of me as I was of him.

With just two weeks to go, my foul mood forced me to consider taking the pills the doctor in Delaware had given me. Maybe I had brought them along with the notion that they might be able to help me. Although skeptical that medication would do any good, I was desperate. I opened the bottle, scooped up a pill, and started to put it in my mouth but then hesitated. Unsure whether I should take a whole pill, I cut it in quarters and then swallowed just one piece. It had no effect. I expected to feel better the next day, but of course, I didn't. *So much for medication working miracles*, I thought and shoved the pills into the bottom of my suitcase without trying them again. Perhaps if I had given the pills a chance to work, the final two weeks wouldn't have been so bad.

While home for the weekend before the last week of traveling, I had another panic attack. It lasted longer than any previous attacks, but I made myself finish the trip. The next week seemed to last forever, but finally, the season ended as we arrived in Cincinnati. As I was preparing to head back to Delaware, one of the other salesmen asked me how I got along traveling. Sheepishly, I told him I thought it was a disaster, and I wanted nothing more to do with Sam. Lowering his voice, he said, "Sam has had a tough life. Not only has he been in trouble before, but his son just got out of prison after committing a robbery where he was shot in the leg. He still walks with a limp."

With the road trip over, I returned to work at the store. The first thing I asked my father was if he knew about Sam's past because I wouldn't have gone if I'd known. Looking right at me, he said, "No. But if I did, I still would've sent you. You needed the experience."

Two or three days later, I overheard my father tell my mother that I was pretty much useless at work. All I did was stare out the front door. According to him I was *not working out*."

CHAPTER 12

Therapy

My mother soon figured out something was wrong with me. Maybe it was the terrible hopelessness she suffered with her facial problem or her own depression that had hampered her for years, but instinctively, she knew she had to get me help. She reached out to her psychiatrist who put me through a series of tests to determine what type of career would be best for me. At that time, there were no therapy sessions planned because no one knew the extent of my mental suffering.

I had little interest in the exams and didn't care about the results. All I wanted to do was to crawl into bed and pull the covers over my head. I needed psychological help but wasn't receiving it.

When the results of my testing came in, a female psychiatrist met with me to go over the results. She made me feel so comfortable that, for the first time, I was honest with myself and told her the results of the tests meant nothing. I just needed someone to talk to. She must have felt my desperation, because she immediately called the front desk to demand an appointment with my psychiatrist for the very next day. Thus, began my lifelong journey into therapy.

The next day, I met with Dr. Rodney Head. He was in his mid-fifties, bald, and chain-smoked like so many of his generation. At first, I was reluctant to tell him how I felt. How could I trust this stranger? As the session progressed, I relaxed a bit, becoming more open and trusting of him. By the end of the third or fourth session, I knew he was going to listen and be able to help me. For the first time in years, I felt hope.

During one of our first sessions, he asked me a question for which I was not prepared. What did I see when I masturbated?

"Having sex with women," I hesitantly answered.

"Good," he replied. "Let's continue."

I guess that eliminated any question of my being a homosexual, but why did it make a difference? Was he going to stop treating me if I was gay? What about the incident in Florida with my homosexual roommate? I walked out without even discussing his sexuality, appearing to be homophobic. I knew I wasn't, and I wanted to ask Dr. Head the relevance of the question, but I was so overcome with feeling nothing that I never did. He never brought it up again.

Doctor Head met with me once a week. No medications were prescribed, as he thought too many of them had bad side effects. He recommended staying the course, allowing time and lots of therapy to do their job. The outcome? No improvement. In fact, I got worse. I soon realized the person I needed most was Lenni, but it was only March. And she was a thousand miles away at Rollins.

CHAPTER 13

Suicidal Ideations

Lenni planned to spend the summer with me in Delaware before returning for her final semester at Rollins. One day in May, her trunk arrived, packed with her belongings. She was to come the following week. Even though I needed her more than ever, the thought of her arrival sparked an onslaught of terrifying images in my mind.

I couldn't stop these images that came out of nowhere. They flooded my consciousness and screeched relentlessly over and over to *get rid of her and tell her to stay home.*

It was as if someone from outside my body was controlling my mind. Unable to resist, I called Lenni and told her not to come. Then I returned her trunk. I was out of control, unaware of what was about to happen. I was sure she was out of my life forever.

On June 9, 1971, I went to the Delaware County pool to swim laps. My actions had scared the shit out of me, so I decided that physical activity would help dull my thoughts. As soon as I hit the water, all I could think of was *Kill yourself! Kill yourself!* Each stroke was agony. Unable to outrun my thoughts, I leapt from the pool, grabbed my towel, and ran to the exit after only two laps. Never had my own mind tried to consistently convince me to end my life. The next day proved to be even worse.

On Saturdays, instead of working at the main store, I opened and closed the *Hook 'N Hanger*, our college-oriented store located down the street. On June 10, I walked in and turned off the alarm, and that's when my mind started to spin out of control once again. I was fighting for survival, fending off orders to kill myself. I quickly grabbed the phone and called Dr. Head, as he was the only one who could save me from myself.

As soon as he answered, I asked if I could see him right away. To my dismay, he responded, "Not today. My daughter is getting married. Can you wait until Monday?"

I shakily answered, "Sure."

I didn't have the courage to insist otherwise. For the rest of the day, it was a desperate fight to keep myself from committing suicide.

On Sunday, June 11, all hell broke loose. All day, I had somehow kept from harming myself. To say it wasn't easy is an understatement. That evening, we were having a barbecue at my parents' house. My sister was at work, but her husband joined us. My task was to grill the burgers. As I was standing in front of the grill ready to flip the burgers, my father pushed me aside saying, "You don't know how to cook good burgers. I'll do it."

I freaked out. Lying on the table next to the grill was a sharp carving knife. Quickly and without thinking, I swooped it up, preparing to stab my father. I told myself to *gut him*.

Suddenly an unexpected calm swept over me. Instead of plunging the knife into my father, my mind's voice of reason screamed, "Stop! Go to Harding Hospital! It's your only chance for survival."

I called my sister at her hospital and told her about the episode. Without hesitation, she called Harding Hospital. They told her to get me there as quickly as possible. Immediately my brother-in-law whisked me into the car and made the twenty-five-minute drive in record time.

CHAPTER 14

Harding Hospital

Harding Hospital was the psychiatric hospital founded by Dr. George T. Harding in 1916. Situated on twenty or more lush, green, wooded acres, it was only fifteen miles south of Delaware. There were several buildings, each with a special name and function. One was for art therapy and another for group therapy. Tennis and basketball courts were located on the front lawn. A gymnasium that also served as a cafeteria was close by. Doctor and staff offices were in the main building, where one-on-one therapy took place. Three housing units for a few hundred patients surrounded the main building.

As soon as we arrived, a nurse and a psychiatrist hustled me into a private room. With my brother-in-law by my side, I went into detail concerning the episode and my constant suicidal ideation. Minutes later, the nurse had me drink a small amount of liquid that caused me to get much-needed sleep over the next two days.

When I awoke, I found myself in a private bedroom just down the hall from the dayroom where all the patients gathered. As I entered the dayroom and surveyed the group, I noticed most of the patients appeared to be ordinary people just like me. I wouldn't describe them as *normal* because if they were, they wouldn't be there. Some were alcoholics, some drug addicts, but the predominant group was mentally ill. We all had our own special problems: schizophrenia, manic depression, multiple personalities, and other horrible disorders.

Later that day, I was summoned to a nearby office. I met with a psychiatrist with whom I discussed at length what I was going

53

through. He was somewhat aloof compared to Dr. Head, so it was difficult to warm up to him. Frankly, I felt he was not as understanding.

After hearing my story, he concluded that I was suffering from depression. He told me not to worry and that I'd be back to normal in approximately four weeks. He couldn't have been more wrong.

The next afternoon, I finally met with Dr. Head. His first question was why I hadn't told him how badly I felt when I had called him the previous Saturday. All I could say was that I didn't want to bother him on his daughter's wedding day. A typical response, as I felt his life was more important than my own.

From then on, I met with him three times a week. Right away, he prescribed Mellaril, a medication used to treat schizophrenia, suicidal ideation, and other mood disorders. I found that it did help control my suicidal thinking. His other recommendation was to start a routine of physical work to keep me both mentally and physically focused, in hopes it would help alleviate my runaway thoughts. I began hauling and spreading stone to create a path through the woods. When it was completed, I helped erect a new basketball backboard.

These chores helped somewhat to curb my anxiety, until I was sent to cut down high weeds in a nearby field. As I swung my sickle, a voice inside my head screamed, "Kill yourself!" over and over all afternoon long. I returned to the dorm and told the nurse I had suicidal thoughts, and she immediately increased the Mellaril dosage to help calm me.

Each morning, patients participated in a class of physical exercises ranging from calisthenics to running laps. Afterward, we would go to art therapy where, depending upon our symptoms, each patient would be prescribed a task. People like me who had anger issues would stand before separate stations backed with metal partitions. On each table would be a hunk of clay. The idea was to slowly mold the clay into a ball and then hurl it against the partition. Each of us began by taking our time to work with the mound and then listlessly toss it against the wall. As time went on, we began throwing it harder, until we were throwing with all our might, screaming and swearing at the top of our lungs. The next step was to slowly ease us down to where we could control our aggression. After days of going through this ritual, a few patients (but unfortunately not all) were better able to control their feelings. Luckily, I was one of the people it helped. At least somewhat.

To people not suffering from mental illness, these activities probably seemed unconventional, if not unnecessary. However, for many of us, they were quite beneficial. I began to feel better, and after a few weeks of treatment, the suicidal thoughts disappeared and never materialized again.

CHAPTER 15

Mr. and Mrs. Wilson

I was hospitalized for a total of three weeks. When I returned home, the first person I went to see was my close friend, David. He was a terrific guy who was the lead in the high school play, *Bye Bye Birdie*, and the singer in a local band. During the summers, we lifeguarded together and even went gigging with *frog*. After college, he followed his dream and moved to Los Angeles to become a comedy writer. His crowning achievement was the creation of the hit series, "Becker," starring Ted Danson. He was the person I would call whenever I was distressed about my father and what he had done. His understanding had been crucial to me throughout my life.

To ease me back into *normal* life, my psychiatrist got me a job as a counselor at a local summer camp for the underprivileged (as if I were in any shape to work with children). Instead of spending time with the kids, I found myself wandering in the woods, crying profusely. At the end of the second day, I decided I wasn't doing anybody any good, so I quit.

When I returned home from camp, I found a bill for $3,000 from Harding Hospital waiting for me. Later that night, I presented the bill to my father. All he said was, "It's your bill. You pay it."

Since I was only making $100 a week, I asked him how that was even possible. He just shrugged his shoulders and walked away. My grandparents had given me $1,500 as a graduation present, so the next day, I sent it to Harding. I paid the remaining balance over the next few years.

I continued to work at Wilson's, but to ease my boredom, I applied for a part-time position as a sportswriter for our local newspaper. I was hired to write about local sports, such as recreational basketball, football, and softball. I found myself to be good at this job. Because of my success, the athletic director for Ohio Wesleyan asked me to be the sports information director for the university. It was also a part-time position but turned out to be an exciting challenge.

I began the job in the fall, during football season. My job was to report on the team's progress, get them as much publicity as possible, and oversee the press box. It was quite fun, as the team proved to be one of the best in the Midwest region. They won all but one of their games. Their talent and success earned them an invitation to the 1971 inaugural Amos Alonzo Stagg Bowl. It was to be played in Columbus, Georgia, on the Saturday after Thanksgiving.

I didn't know it, but my friend Mike had been asked by Lenni to keep her informed about how I was doing. One evening about three weeks before the bowl game, I overheard Mike on the phone with her. She knew nothing about my hospital stay or anything else that had transpired through the summer. I asked Mike to let me speak to her. We reconnected with a friendly conversation, and I told her about my upcoming trip to Georgia. To my surprise, she told me her roommate was from Columbus, Georgia, and had invited her to go home with her for Thanksgiving.

I couldn't believe it. If I were a religious person, I would say it was God's plan. Since I'm not, I chalked it up to pure luck and some sort of sign that perhaps Lenni and I could work things out after all.

We met in a sleazy nine-dollar-a-night motel the night before the game. Instantly both of us knew we wanted to get back together, but she said there would be no intimacy unless I told her what had happened to me. I told her everything.

I watched her as she listened and absorbed what I was telling her. Her reaction was one of understanding and compassion. After two wonderful nights together, we vowed to keep in touch.

Even though we lost the bowl game, I was asked to write a story titled, *The Making of a Championship Football Team* for Wesleyan's winter addition of its alumni magazine. A few days later, the head of the publicity department and the athletic director came to see me while I was working at the store. Having read the piece I had written and loved the positive press I had gotten for Ohio Wesleyan, they offered to send me to Ohio University's School of Sports Management. When finished with the program, I could return to Wesleyan as its full-time sports information director. It sounded fantastic, and I wanted to accept. But I still suffered from depression and was afraid that if I left the security of my home base, the suicidal ideations would return, and I would fall apart once again. Safety was more important than doing something I really would have enjoyed. Reluctantly, I turned them down. I was just too afraid of being in a new environment all alone. Instead, I focused my efforts on my blossoming relationship with Lenni.

Lenni graduated from Rollins with a degree in fine arts in December of 1971. While deciding what to do, she returned to Philadelphia and got a job as a server at a neighborhood bar and grill. I continued to work at the store, plus the part-time SID job for Ohio Wesleyan.

In March, I drove to Philadelphia to bring Lenni back to Delaware with me. She was going to get her own apartment and find a job. On the afternoon we were to depart, her mother scowled and grumbled, "We never should have sent you to that college. All you did was learn to drink and fornicate." With that gracious goodbye, we headed west to Ohio.

At that time, I was still going to therapy and had started trying various medications to see if any of them eased the depression. Nothing worked. They either made me sick as a dog, hyped me up, or had no effect at all. Luckily, Lenni was around to give me support.

Six months later in early summer, Lenni and I were visiting my mother when she asked if we had plans to marry. She and my brother were going on a trip and wanted to know before she left, so plans could be made. Looking at each other, we said, "Why not?"

Not the most romantic of proposals, but we had decided the timing was right.

We gave Lenni's parents five weeks' notice to find a venue for only close relatives and friends. Given the fact that I wasn't Jewish and her parents were not thrilled with our marriage, we didn't want any more drama than necessary. Most places had been booked months in advance, so arrangements were made for the ceremony to be held in August at the Cherry Hill Inn in neighboring New Jersey. Everything went much better than expected. Her parents appeared to accept the situation and were wonderful hosts. They met my family for the first time, and everything went well.

Following the reception, we drove an hour to Atlantic City to spend our first night as Mr. and Mrs. Wilson. At that time, I was extremely excited about spending my life with Lenni. Even though I had put her through hell, all of that was in the past, and the future looked great. The next morning, Lenni got up early and headed to the beach, while I lingered in bed. Out of nowhere, a familiar voice screamed in my head, "You should not have gotten married!"

Relentlessly, I pondered over the *mistake* I had made. I sprang from the bed and hustled toward the beach. As soon as I reached Lenni, I blurted out what I was thinking.

This was her first encounter with me being so irrational. Her reaction? Stunned silence. It was her first time seeing me being demonized by my own thoughts. After a while, as I laid down in the warm sand, I was able to settle down and promised Lenni I would always let her know when I experienced these thoughts. After that, the destructive thoughts subsided.

CHAPTER 16

McCormick Ranch

Later that week, we returned to Delaware. I continued to work in my father's clothing store for the next six months or so, until I couldn't stand it any longer. I despised working with my father and was so bored that I began to feel like a prisoner. Throwing caution to the wind, Lenni and I decided to leave Delaware and head West. On a freezing, snowy winter day in January of 1973, we loaded our yellow Mercury Capri and took off. One of my intentions was to secure a job as an assistant golf pro in a place that had good weather year-round—maybe San Diego. We had no idea what our future held for us or where we would wind up, but both of us were extremely excited about the adventure.

After a few days drive and over one thousand eight hundred miles, we arrived in Tucson, Arizona, to a wonderful seventy degrees. We didn't think much of the city, so we headed north to Phoenix. Ever since I had attended the golf school near there, I kept thinking what a great place it was. As soon as we arrived and saw the swaying palm trees with mountains in the background, most notably Camelback Mountain, we knew Phoenix was where we wanted to settle.

At that time, Phoenix was a town of approximately 400,000 residents. It was difficult to find affordable apartments because the "snowbirds" rented them for the winter season. We managed to locate a new complex just north of Thomas Road on 44th Street—not far from Camelback Road. I spent the first month applying for golf jobs. With the help of the Ohio Wesleyan golf coach, who had taken me to the teacher's golf school in nearby Cave Creek, I was chosen for the position of assistant golf pro at McCormick Ranch Golf Club in Scottsdale, a course that had opened the previous year. My salary was $500 per month. With our rent of $175 per month, things would be tight, but at least I'd be doing something I wanted to do.

The major problem was that I hadn't played much golf recently, and now my job was to dazzle local enthusiasts with my ability to play, run the pro shop, and give lessons. Would disastrous mental issues that inhibited my ability to perform at a high level still plague me? I didn't have long to find out.

One day following my morning shift, I was asked by three excellent players to join their group. Nervously, I accepted. Bets were placed, and the game was on. It was my first time playing in a long time. I envisioned myself playing as I had when I was in complete control of my game.

As I strode to the first tee, I realized this was my opportunity to prove I could still play well. All eyes were on me as I placed my golf ball on the tee, took a couple of practice swings, and lined up to hit a high draw (a shot that moves from right to left.)

Every good golfer could instantly feel when he's made a good swing and hit the ball exactly as he wanted. I was anticipating that as I took my first swing. Instead, it felt as if I was swinging a sledge-hammer. The ball sailed off the face of the club as if I had just hit a ball of mud. It traveled one hundred fifty yards, landing well off the fairway. Ruefully, I slammed my driver into my bag, got into the cart, and headed off to hit my next shot. The golfer sitting next to me then quietly said, "Maybe we should forget about playing for money."

Three hours later, the round was over with each of the three guys shooting in the seventies. I finished with a ninety-one. Frustrated and embarrassed, I slinked into the clubhouse and slumped down at my locker. How could I be a golf professional when I couldn't even play like a pro?

Stan, the club's head pro, came in, sat down beside me, and then asked why I was so upset. I couldn't help myself and told him not only about my fears of not being able to succeed in golf but also what I had been through, including my hospital stay and past suicidal thoughts. He listened intently, then got up, and walked away, saying nothing. He was around thirty-five, had been a pro for ten years, but was not a great golfer. In fact, I doubted if he could break eighty. It never entered my mind that he would hold against me what I had divulged to him. Later that summer, I found out how wrong I had been.

Each day, the course was filled with golfers from all over the world taking advantage of Phoenix's great weather. I had little time to be bored, let alone dwell on any negative thoughts. When the weather went from a delightful seventy to eighty degrees to an unbearable one hundred five to one hundred fifteen degrees, most golfers returned to their hometowns until October. The number of golfers playing at McCormick Ranch from October through May dwindled in the summer months from an average of twenty-four per hour to only thirty per day. With little to do, boredom, my old nemesis returned. This time, however, I was determined to squash it, as I knew the perfect weather would eventually return and with it, hordes of golfers. Hopefully, I could spend time working on my game to get it back to where it should be.

To bring in some summer business, Stan got a contract to host one of golf's first United States mini tours. It was to start in late June and last six weeks. Wannabe professional golfers from both all over the country and outside the United States descended upon Scottsdale for a chance to be recognized as possible tour candidates. One such player even arrived by helicopter. After shooting an eighty-five the first day, he departed not by helicopter but by taxi.

The night before the tour was to begin, the club held a banquet for the participants. It took place at a well-known restaurant on Pinnacle Peak Mountain. It had a reputation as the best place to go without having to wear a tie. In fact, if you wore one, a server would come by, snip it in half, and hang it on the wall with hundreds of others.

It was during this dinner that Stan introduced himself and his staff, lavishing praise on each member, except me. He skipped me altogether. I realized my admission to him about my mental problems had been a mistake. Like many others, he evidently viewed those with mental struggles as weak. More than that, he viewed me as someone to be avoided. I was stunned. I had no idea he would turn on me just because of the stigma surrounding mental illness. Did he want me to quit?

I hadn't suffered any severe depression attacks for several months, but the head pro's attitude, along with my own misgivings, created one. After suffering a sleepless night, I called in sick the next day and saw a doctor who prescribed Navane, an antipsychotic drug, to help me gain control of myself. Fortunately, it helped within a couple of days so I could go back to work. However, the damage had been done. In my absence, my boss had one of the other assistants rearrange how I had displayed the different golf essentials in the pro shop. He most likely thought my inability to work was the beginning of a pattern brought on by my mental illness. I realized my stint as a golf pro was in jeopardy. It wasn't enough for me to be able to just play the game like a pro—I had to be able to teach the game, as well. Evidently, Stan decided if I wasn't right mentally, I couldn't do either.

Instead of speaking directly to Stan about my concerns and trying to salvage the situation, I gave up and decided it was time for me to move on. The only problem was I didn't have another job waiting for me.

CHAPTER 17

The New Store

While I was dealing with my problems at McCormick Ranch, my mother called to tell me my father had just purchased a men's clothing store located in downtown Worthington, about fifteen miles south of Delaware. I was familiar with the store. It had originally been located near the Ohio State campus in Columbus but was forced to relocate after race riots gripped the city in the sixties and early seventies. The store had catered to very conservative professors, lawyers, and businessmen, but, once in Worthington, the demographics were not the same.

Most people were now caught up in the fashions of the seventies. Men quit wearing three button, soft shoulder conservative suits and took on the look of the times. Suits had wide lapels on the jackets. Slacks were flared at the bottom, and many guys wore silk shirts with loud prints. It was a great new fashion era.

My father wanted the new store to remain the same as before, but my mother said I would have total control of its future if I chose to run it. To me, that meant I could transform it into a more up-to-date operation. After discussing it with Lenni, I resigned my position at McCormick Ranch, and we headed back to Ohio.

An additional bonus was that I would be working *for* my father and not directly *with* him. As far as salary, Mom said our move would be paid for, and I would be well compensated—a good thing because we were struggling financially. I felt upbeat about the challenge. I'd be able to grow the business and be in a better financial position. I had made a huge mistake by not confirming all this with my father. My mother had been the one with whom I made the deal. Unfortunately, it didn't take long to discover how big a mistake it was.

My father summoned me to his office the day after we returned to Delaware to discuss the plans for the new store. The first thing he said was that the business couldn't afford to reimburse our entire moving expenses, but he would pay half. Then he informed me that my salary would be far below what my mother had told me. He saved the worst news for last: instead of me being in charge, he had convinced the previous owner of the store to remain as the manager. The son of a bitch had screwed me again.

I had no choice but to accept the terms. Had I been naïve to think he would be different? Perhaps, but I never dreamed my own father would treat me this way.

The new store was a disaster from the very beginning. No changes were made. Few customers walked in, and the so-called client lists my father had purchased were useless. Just two years after adding it to the Wilson empire, the store was liquidated and shuttered forever. For me, depression had been my constant companion ever since I realized we should never have come back. Anger crept up so badly that many times, while alone at the store, I would hurl things down the steps into the basement. In fact, when I couldn't get the Christmas tree to stand straight, I took it out of its stand, threw it on the floor, and began beating it with a hammer, screaming every expletive I had in my arsenal. This was reminiscent of how I had reacted as a teenager. If I hit too many bad golf shots, I would throw my club. On one occasion, after missing the green on a par three hole, I began slamming my wedge into a nearby trash can over and over.

I was out of control.

CHAPTER 18

Scioto Country Club

One day, shortly before closing the Worthington store, a neighbor of ours asked me to play golf with him and a couple of his buddies. He knew I had been a golf professional, and he wanted to see how I would fare against the three of them. Even though I was scared shitless, I accepted the challenge. We were going to play at the famed Scioto Country Club in Columbus, the home course of professional golfer, Jack Nicklaus, and it was going to be the first time I had hit a golf ball in two years.

My three opponents were good golfers and knew Scioto like the back of their hands. It was a chilly October day, laced with the threat of rain. One of the guys picked his ball out of the hat first, so he was number one on the tee. He nailed a two hundred fifty-yard shot right down the middle. The next guy picked his ball up, sauntered to the tee, and smacked a beauty down the right side of the fairway. My neighbor was next. He had a distinct *waggle* as he set up, but it all came together in the end. And his ball flew past the first player. Then it was my turn. I had a great swing and always looked perfect when taking a few practice swings, but that's where it ended. With sweat pouring from every pore, I took a smooth, natural swing and hit a shot that never got off the ground and traveled only about one hundred twenty-five yards.

Having just hacked my tee shot, I couldn't contain my anxiety. No matter how I tried, nothing went right. I couldn't hit my woods and irons nor could I chip or putt. It proved to be the worst round of golf I had ever played, coming home at 103 strokes. Worse than that, I had worn out my welcome with my three opponents, each having shoot less than eighty-five, because they had expected me to be fantastic. "We don't want to play with you again," they said with their eyes. They didn't.

Following my disastrous play at Scioto, I shoved my clubs in the corner of the garage and didn't play again for a long time. I didn't know it at the time, but my inability to play good golf would plague me for years to come, even among close friends.

Every November, some friends of mine from Delaware and I would travel to Florida for four or five days of golf, food, and booze. It was always a great time, but worrying about my game caused me to be so anxious I couldn't enjoy playing. I shot terrible scores, making for a miserable time on the course. It wasn't just when we went on these trips that I played horribly—it was anytime I tried to play golf. Finally, I gathered up all my golf equipment and took it to a local golf outlet and sold everything for $40. I never played again. All because I couldn't forgive myself for cheating fifty years before.

CHAPTER 19

Jami

There was one real bright spot in my life: the first of our three daughters, Jami, was born (ironically on my father's birthday) in 1974. I vividly remember watching the Ohio State-Michigan football game in Lenni's hospital room with Jami snuggled next to her mother. The OSU Buckeyes won twelve to ten—another reason it was a great day.

In the Jewish faith, it was a tradition to name a newborn after someone who had passed. At first we were going to name her Gayle but decided to name her in honor of Lenni's paternal grandmother, Julia. Lenni's parents flew out two weeks later to meet their new granddaughter, and a remarkable thing happened. Her mom took me aside and said, "Welcome to our family." It had taken two years for her to realize I wasn't so bad after all. From then on, she and I became the best of friends.

One day, when Jami was three, Lenni dropped a couple of pans while fixing dinner in the kitchen. They made a loud bang when they hit the floor. Jami, who was sitting on the floor next to Lenni, didn't react to the thunderous sound. Worried, Lenni picked up one of the pans, stood behind Jami, and gave it a whack with a spoon. Jami didn't even flinch. I was in the family room watching TV when Lenni yelled for me. She repeated the action with the pan and spoon, but still Jami didn't respond. It was the first sign that there was something wrong with Jami's hearing. We took her to an audiologist in downtown Columbus who confirmed Jami had substantial hearing loss, and the only thing that would help was hearing aids. Lenni's brother had developed hearing loss in first grade and wore two hearing aids, so Lenni was familiar with the situation. Even so, she was still devastated that Jami would suffer the same fate.

The first time Jami walked out of the audiologist's office wearing the hearing aids, she held on to our hands tightly, as the loud traffic noise frightened her. On the ride home, she had us turn down the radio because it was too loud. We looked at each other in amazement, thrilled that she could hear.

It didn't take long for Jami to get used to them. It became routine to put them in each morning. The transformation was incredible. For the first time, she heard our voices and everything else around her. I had been reading her bedtime stories for years, and now she was so much more attentive.

There was one drawback: As she grew older, she became self-conscious when other kids noticed the objects behind her ears. She knew she was different and was embarrassed. When the owner of the Strand Theater heard about Jami's disability, he purchased a separate hearing device, which he installed in the balcony at his own expense. All she had to do was go up to the balcony and slip it on, and she could hear the movie just fine. However, that made her feel awkward, and she refused to use it.

Jami's hearing challenges affected me deeply. Not only did I worry about her being bullied horribly by other kids, but I had no idea what problems she would face throughout her life. How would she handle her situation emotionally?

To my wonderment, she handled her disability quite well. She made wonderful friends, got excellent grades because of hard work, and became a top player on the girl's high school tennis team. The only time she hit a rough patch was when she was in her early teens. I don't know how much of her hearing problem played a role, if at all, nor do I know if she felt neglected by all the attention we paid to her younger sister, Cari, and her gymnastics, but she became quite depressed for a spell. The thought of her having to face similar emotions to what I was going through saddened me, and I felt it was my fault. I was sure she had inherited depression from me.

CHAPTER 20

Lazarus

Because of the Worthington store's failure, I was forced to return to the main store in Delaware. I persevered and tried to make the best of it. With financial help from Lenni's family, we were able to purchase a house in Delaware, cementing our commitment to the community.

Once again, working near my father proved to be an untenable situation. A year later, I resigned my position as the *errand boy*. It was time to venture into another facet of retailing. I had my sights set on joining one of the major department stores in downtown Columbus as a buyer, thinking it would be a much faster pace and an environment in which I could grow and prosper.

When I sent out my resume to Schottenstein's and F&R Lazarus department stores, I received offers from both companies. After all, Wilson's was well known throughout Ohio as a great store, and I was well suited for both positions. I chose to enter the Lazarus Executive Merchandising program, while I worked at its flagship store in Columbus, even though Schottenstein's had offered me more money. Schottenstein's was a very successful discount operation, but I was swayed by the more prestigious Lazarus.

Almost from day one, the pressure was too much for me. I had been on Navane for a while, and it helped relieve my anger issues but did little to help my depression. The fierce competition and backstabbing among coworkers, along with my failure in golf, the store closure, and the disastrous year and half working with my father had taken its toll. The rapid heartbeat, insomnia, body aches, and loneliness returned with a vengeance. Even though I had a wonderful wife, a beautiful daughter, and another child on the way, I felt as though each day was too much to handle. I was adrift in a huge department store teeming with people, and from day one, I didn't belong.

The buyer of men's slacks was to train me to be a future buyer. Instead, he made things even more miserable. From the beginning, he did little to guide me through the workings of the company. In fact, he relegated me to the position of salesperson and pretty much ignored me. He taught me nothing, so I complained to those above him. He threw a tantrum and told me to stay away from him, thus controlling the direction of my future with Lazarus. A pattern was developing, but I was unwilling to accept that I always reacted to a difficult situation by blaming the person in charge. This would hamper me throughout my future as I struggled to handle delicate situations.

Working at Lazarus continued to be a nightmare that caused my anxiety to spiral out of control. I went through each day under so much stress that I thought I was going to lose it. Thankfully, I never contemplated suicide again, but I was desperate to get away from there, so I made the same stupid decision I'd made when things got tough at McCormick Ranch.

Without much thought and regard for myself or my family, I called my father and begged him to take me back. I was at a new low. Anything would be better than what I was going through at Lazarus. It's funny how I was able to convince myself that things would be better working with my father again. All I was doing was trading one painful experience for another. As usual, I didn't think the situation through completely.

Even though the problems at the store were just as bad as before, I was able to keep my home life separate. Just prior to leaving Lazarus in 1977, our middle daughter, Cari, was born. We had moved into a spec home in Delaware and discovered our neighborhood had wonderful people who became good friends.

CHAPTER 21

Out of Our Lives

Our next-door neighbors became our best friends. Our kids grew up together, and, for the most part, we had similar interests and beliefs. The dad, Joe, was a principal at a local high school, and his wife, Linda, was a math teacher at a different high school.

For over twenty years, we walked in and out of each other's homes at will and went on vacations together. Lenni and I spent more time with them than all the rest of our friends put together. It was as if we were one big happy family. The relationship was as good as it gets. Then, in 2001, things began to change as they transitioned from best friends to acquaintances.

Lenni wasn't sure why the change occurred, but I was. One of their daughters had a growing relationship with a boy from Delaware since eighth grade. Eventually, they got married. Our best friends soon began spending their time with his parents rather than us. Suddenly they had no time for us. No longer did we attend basketball games or go to movies with them. Everything changed, and it was as if the lights were turned off, never to brighten again.

I took it much harder than Lenni. In my mind, I felt deserted. Over the years, we had welcomed them into our family, and now they were all but out of our lives. Luckily, I had added the medication Paxil to my daily routine a couple of years before. I had also switched from Lithium to Lamictal because of the damage Lithium had done to my kidneys, which rounded out my *cocktail*. The change proved effective, as I managed to stay afloat during these trying times. In the end, we built a custom home in the country, and our neighbors moved to a new home fifteen miles away. We rarely saw Joe and Linda after that.

CHAPTER 22

Cari

Our second daughter, Cari, was born in 1977, right after I went to work at Lazarus. She was bald and had the lungs of a screeching banshee. From the beginning, she proved to be a good athlete. Every spring at her elementary school, they would hold a day of track-and-field events. She excelled at all of them and still hold the records in some. Academically, she was at the top of her class. What I didn't realize was that she worried compulsively even at a young age. As she grew older, her worrying worsened, to where whenever I was flying, she couldn't sleep for fear the plane would crash.

Much later, following the birth of her first child, Cari was overcome with postpartum depression. It was a harrowing time for her and led her into her own world of therapy and medication. Once again, I pondered whether she had inherited her nightmare from me.

At the age of three, Cari expressed a desire to start gymnastics at the Delaware Recreation Center. She proved to be a natural. Two years later, she joined a private gymnastics club, Buckeye Gymnastics, where she started working out with other girls who excelled at the sport at an early age. Two months after joining, she competed in her first meet. From then on, it was three hours of practice each weekday, followed with a meet on Sunday. Each day, I would pick her up from school and drive her to the gym, which was forty-five minutes away, watch her practice, and drive her home afterward. Sundays meant a meet somewhere in Columbus or cities up to two hours away. On special occasions, Cari would even compete in meets held out of the state. Her specialties were the beam and the floor. In 1990, she won the beam competition at a national meet in Niagara Falls, New York.

To say Cari's plunge into the sport affected the entire family was an understatement. Our entire lives revolved around her and gymnastics. That meant Jami and later Casi, our youngest daughter who was born in 1980, were dragged along for the ride. For Lenni and me, it was hectic and fun. We made a lot of new friends and loved watching the competition. For Jami and Casi, not so much. They were forced to go to almost all of Cari's meets, and at times, I sensed they felt neglected.

Then, without warning when she was thirteen, Cari quit gymnastics. She'd had enough of the rigorous workouts and the time away from her school friends. It was time to be a regular kid. What I didn't realize was that Cari was under extreme pressure to succeed and that, coupled with her own fears and doubts, it was unnerving. In the years to come, like me, she would be plagued with her own mental struggles. Once again, I had the feeling that her depression was my fault. She got it from me. However, it was now time to focus our attention on the entire family.

CHAPTER 23

Beth Tikvah

No matter how hard my parents tried to influence our lives, Lenni and I wouldn't let them. They had started a new church and wanted us to benefit from a life devoted to Jesus. However, we went in a different direction.

In Judaism, children born to a Jewish mother are considered Jewish. It doesn't matter if the father isn't Jewish. Lenni and I joined Beth Tikvah, a synagogue in Worthington. Although I was not going to change from being an atheist, I supported Lenni's decision.

My atheism came about because God never helped me with my bipolar disorder. Also, I believed that if there was someone out there, he had turned his back on the entire world and its horrific problems. Bad people continued to get away with their hellish acts, while normal, everyday people suffered. In other words, there was no higher power watching over the world. Lenni agreed but would not go as far as to say she was an atheist.

A month later, on Christmas Day, we gathered around the dinner table with Sandy, her husband Bill, Mom, Dad, and Tommy. I made the mistake of announcing our new affiliation with Beth Tikvah. As Lenni and I smiled, there was a collective gasp from the others. Not surprisingly, they were stunned, acting as if we had committed a mortal sin from which there was no escape. Lenni and I looked on, knowing we had opened a festering wound.

It didn't matter that my wife was Jewish. My parents, Sandy, Bill, and Tommy believed that anyone who wasn't Christian did not meet their high standards. Later, when I was talking on the phone to Tommy about us joining the temple, he referred to Lenni as a *gold digger*, meaning she had married me for my family's supposed fortune. That was unbelievable because Lenni's father, Farrel, was far more successful. He, his dad, and brother owned and operated fifteen restaurants in Philadelphia. Named for Farrel's father, the restaurants were called *Dewey's*.

Established in the 1950s, they were an early version of McDonald's, strategically placed on all the right corners in Philadelphia and specializing in hamburgers and milkshakes. In 1970, a full meal at Dewey's was less than a dollar. The business was a huge success, but none of that mattered to my parents. All that mattered was that Lenni was Jewish and didn't believe Jesus was God's son. My father took me aside and told me Lenni was going to hell. From then on, there was no repairing my relationship with my parents, and Lenni all but ignored them from then on.

CHAPTER 24

Bipolar Disorder

As Dr. Head and I continued to meet regularly, he prescribed various antidepressants, each of which had little effect. Finally, in 1978, eight years after I was first diagnosed, he suggested that perhaps I was suffering from manic depression—also known as bipolar disorder. This refers to disorders of mood involving alternating episodes of depression and mania. According to The National Institute of Mental Health Disorders, approximately 26 percent or ninety-two million Americans suffer from some type of mental illness. Bipolar disorder is among the most common with just over 2 percent of adults effected. The average onset age is twenty-five with 83 percent considered severe. The condition is treatable, but not curable.

There are two main types of bipolar disorder. The first, bipolar disorder type I, is when the patient experiences a manic state in which they will be on a tremendous high that can last hours, days, or even months. During this time, they will feel invincible, often causing them to throw caution to the wind and risk everything. Without warning, they will then crash into a state of depression. The second type, bipolar disorder type II, which I battle, is when the patient experiences deep levels of depression for days or months. Suicidal ideation often occurs during these times. Patients have described a feeling as if nothing matters in their lives. There is no joy or purpose. This may be followed by a manic state in which the patient feels better but is not a true high. This state is known as hypomania.

It is a mistake to think that people with bipolar disorder are crazy or that they should be institutionalized. No one who has not experienced deep depression can know what it is like. No matter how vividly a person describes to someone what they are going through, no one can feel an experience foreign to them. It is very difficult to comprehend the depths of depression that one can suffer if you have not suffered it yourself.

Doctor Head asked me to try Lithium, a medication that had a great track record treating this disorder. He said it would probably take a few weeks to kick in, but it was worth a shot. He was wrong. It took only two days.

It was a new beginning. I hadn't felt that good in years, and my mind was clearer. A few days later, I went back to see him, and he was amazed at how quickly it had begun to work. He apologized for misdiagnosing my condition and not trying the drug earlier. One thought did nag at me, though. Why had Dr. Head waited so long? None of the other medications worked, so why had I had to suffer for so long before he tried Lithium? And would I have made all those insane decisions if my depression had been better handled? So many consequential acts had transpired that might have been avoided. Doctor Head told me he was concerned about a known side effect—kidney problems—if Lithium was used over a long period of time. I would have to be screened every six months, but I didn't care. I was feeling better, and that was all that mattered. I was on the mend, so I decided not to look back. What was done was done.

On Lithium, I was able to sleep through the night. The anger subsided, and I hadn't suffered any recent panic attacks. I still had both negative and racing thoughts, continued to be impulsive, and making informed decisions was out of the question. But I had much improved.

I was feeling so good, I even thought about repairing my relationship with my father. That is, until he struck again: this time at the expense of Sandy and Bill.

CHAPTER 25

Insurance

My grandfather had spent thirty or forty years accumulating several properties of great value in downtown Delaware. I oversaw maintaining them as well as collecting the rental fees. As president of the real estate company we had set up, my father made any monetary decisions, including which insurance company would insure the properties.

For a few years, Bill had worked in the office of Wilson's in addition to selling clothing. He, too, had trouble getting along with my father and finally left to go into the insurance business with a good friend. Knowing he was starting from scratch, I told him to bid on a new policy for our properties, as renewal was fast approaching. He could certainly use the business.

The current insurance company and my brother-in-law's company both submitted proposals. The coverage was virtually identical, but my brother-in-law's proposal was substantially lower in cost. It seemed like a no-brainer to me, so I suggested to my father that we go with Bill's insurance company.

Without skipping a beat, my father informed me we would be staying with the current company. His rationale? He was good friends with the owner and didn't want to upset him. Hurting his daughter and son-in-law obviously didn't matter. To him, it was simply good business. Right then, I realized how little regard he had for anyone in our family. It was all about how the community perceived him. From that point forward, I lost respect for him. I decided I would always make my own family my number one priority.

CHAPTER 26

Casi

1980 brought the arrival of our third daughter, Casi. She came into the world with a full head of hair and the facial features of an Eskimo. Right away, she showed a thirst for knowledge. Growing up, she read all the time and absorbed everything she could. She loved sports cars, and pictures of Lamborghinis adorned the walls of her room. She was not as athletic as Jami and Cari, but we convinced her to go out for the softball team. When she became the leading base stealer, we adorned her with the moniker of *sticks*—more for her spindly legs than her speed.

After listening to Lenni and I rave about our time in Arizona, she decided she wanted to go to college there. Following a quick trip to the University of Arizona and Arizona State, she selected ASU as the place for her. Early in the school year, she met and almost immediately fell in love with Ryan, who, to our dismay, was a Michigan Wolverine fan. As steadfast Ohio State Buckeye enthusiasts, Lenni and I hassled him during game days. At their wedding, Buckeyes and Wolverines sat apart, but we all managed to have a wonderful time.

It was during the preparation for the wedding that Lenni and I realized Casi was suffering from pent-up anger. When their boxer, Rosco, got into the stash of M&M party favors and ate them, she went off the deep end. It was much more than just wedding jitters. After a while, she was able to calm down, and the wedding went off without a hitch. But I worried that she had inherited the anger from me. I was three for three.

CHAPTER 27

Was I Lying

During the eighties, with our family complete, I enjoyed spending time with the kids and had an abundance of friends. Lenni and I would go to the movies a couple of times a week, and, except for the constant aggravation at work, I was doing a lot better. I still had to deal with one disturbing thing: Every time I took a knife out of the kitchen drawer, the thought of stabbing Lenni would creep into my mind, just as it had with my father years before. But why was it happening? It wasn't to the level as it had been when I previously wanted to stab my father, but it was unnerving to say the least.

After this occurred several times, I told Dr. Head about it. His advice was for me to tell Lenni what I was thinking and to ensure her she was safe. Unsure of how she would react, I went ahead and told her. She had seen me through a variety of mental flare-ups, so neither of us were surprised that she reacted calmly, thanked me for sharing, and kept her thoughts to herself. The relief of sharing my feelings with her was enormous—so much so that the desire to stab her soon evaporated. Doctor Head and I never discussed my irrational thoughts again, but, twenty-five years later, my new trauma psychologist suggested I had suffered from a form of obsessive-compulsive disorder or OCD. It abated when I confronted the compulsion by verbalizing it to Lenni.

One day, at the beginning of a session with Dr. Head, I tried to talk to him about the rape I had experienced as a kid. As traumatizing as it was, I managed to say out loud that I had been molested. It was the first time I had ever spoken to anyone about the incident. He looked at me and then asked, "How are you feeling today?"

Dumbfounded, I answered, "Okay, but did you hear what I just said?"

"Yes, but how are you feeling *today*?"

That was it. Discussion over. It was as if he thought I was lying. Here I had garnered up the courage to talk about the scariest time of my youth, and he totally ignored it. "What the fuck?" I asked myself. Why would I bring it up if it wasn't important? Perhaps I should have walked out on Dr. Head right then, but I didn't. I was too stunned.

After that, I didn't bring the issue up again until about 1995 when I was seeing a new psychologist. To my astonishment, she dismissed the incident right away too. It was as if both thought that a man couldn't be raped or that I was lying. Either way, they let me down.

Finally, twenty years later, in 2015, I told Lenni. She was extremely compassionate, and we talked about it well into the night. For me, it felt as if a huge burden had been lifted from my shoulders. Perhaps if Dr. Head and the other therapist had helped me through the memory, I would have overcome the fallout much sooner.

CHAPTER 28

Buyout

In 1986, after eight tumultuous years at the store sparring with my father, I attempted to buy him out. I presented him with a plan that would be favorable to both of us. Over the next several years, I would pay him monthly to cover the purchase price of the business. As he wasn't ready to fully retire, I would pay him extra to work specified periods throughout the year. He and my mother would be able to spend as much time as they wanted in the Cayman Islands, where they had a second home. I would be in charge, and he would be semiretired. His only obligations were to guarantee he would transition his many customers to me and work at the store as scheduled.

Instead of accepting my offer, Dad took me to Cleveland to meet with a man who specialized in family business succession. It was a good meeting, leading us to believe that we were on the right path to allow him to retire financially secure while I would run the business. However, it didn't take long for Dad to show his true colors. He had his attorney draw up a contract that made it appear as if he were giving me the business. He said it was for tax purposes. He put many restrictions on what direction I could take the business and required me to pay off a large loan he had taken out with my grandmother. One more thing: If I were to die, the business would revert to my siblings instead of Lenni, as she was not a blood relative. It was apparent to me that she was not considered *family* because she was Jewish. Right away, I refused and threatened to quit.

A week later, through my attorney, I received a revised contract. A longtime friend, my attorney told me to reject it, but I knew that since Dad had removed the stipulation about the business not going to Lenni, he wouldn't accept further changes. In fact, it was clear I had to end our business relationship now, or it would never happen. So I signed the contract with the provision he would officially retire two years later. During that time, he and my mother would spend January through May in Grand Cayman.

As my attorney had predicted, it was a huge mistake. My father made no effort to help me retain his customers after he retired. In fact, one of his golf buddies called me to inform me that no one from Marion, where most of Dad's customers lived, would shop with me.

"Why?" I asked.

"Because your father said you forced him out of the business," he answered.

From that moment on, I knew the chances of Wilson's survival was in jeopardy. Fifty percent of our business came from Marion, and just as predicted, most of them didn't shop with us any longer. But there was a far larger problem coming in the not-too-distant future. One that was directly caused by one of my medications.

CHAPTER 29

Blepharospasm

For years, I had noticed that when I drove for a few hours, I would have problems keeping my eyes open. It was an incidental problem, so I ignored it. One day, I was driving locally and had only been in the car for a short while when suddenly I couldn't control my eyelids. They kept opening and closing uncontrollably. Alarmed, I made an appointment with my cousin, who was an ophthalmologist. As the condition got worse, especially when I was exposed to sunlight, my cousin failed to discover what was causing the problem.

Finally, eight months later, he confirmed that I was suffering from tardive dyskinesia, a disorder that results in involuntary, repetitive body movements. In this case, it was my eyelids. Worse than blinking, they spasmed uncontrollably as if I were constantly winking at someone. It was debilitating. The only time it stopped was when I was sleeping.

The eyelid condition was known as blepharospasm. Leave it to me to get something that usually occurs in older women. There was no cure, but Botox could possibly provide some relief. At that time, it was in the trial stages to determine if it was safe to use. I was willing to try anything, so I agreed to be a guinea pig.

My cousin prescribed a series of ten shots around my eyes. The thought of the shots freaked me out, but what else could I do? I couldn't live with the spasms, so I went ahead with the procedure. It really wasn't painful, as they used extremely small needles. Though it took several weeks to get the Botox dosage to a level where it was effective, it worked, and I had no side effects. I would have to repeat the treatment every three months as the Botox wore off over time. All that was left was to determine what caused the disorder.

After further investigation, it was determined that my condition was a result of taking Navane for fifteen years. However, stopping Navane, the medication that kept my anger in check, presented a new problem. What would happen if I stopped taking it? Would the anger come storming back? Was there a replacement drug I could take that wouldn't produce the same effect?

After consulting with my psychiatrist, he concluded that any antipsychotic drug would have the same result. If I went off Navane, the spasms most likely wouldn't diminish. The thought of being overcome with uncontrollable anger or falling into depression again was unnerving, to say the least. My options were continue taking Navane along with the Botox shot or stop the Navane and suffer the consequences. I chose the Botox. Then I tried to see Dr. Head.

CHAPTER 30

Quack

At the same time, I was struggling with blepharospasm, I began ruminating—worrying constantly. I believed that if I said or did anything that might possibly offend or hurt someone, it would ruin their life. On and on, over and over I would tell myself how horrible I had been. For example, I made the decision to change my grandmother's accountant. Immediately, I assumed I had thrown her into bankruptcy, and she would be ruined. I worried until the new accountant assured me that her account was under control. That problem solved, I went on to the next problem, and the next. It was a continuous nightmare that proved to be one of the worst aspects of my bipolar disorder.

To get help, I called Dr. Head. His secretary advised me he had suffered a heart attack and would not be available for several weeks, if not months. Shaken, I got in touch with a friend of mine who was a psychologist. He referred me to a psychiatrist who could see if I needed a change in medication.

Lenni and I went to see this new psychiatrist the next week. After a lengthy discussion, he advised me to throw away all my current medications and replace them with a new breakthrough medication that would solve my mental anguish. He wrote out a prescription for Desyrel, told me to think about it, and said it would change my life forever. I was desperate, so I decided to do as he said.

After picking up the new medication and trusting the psychiatrist's advice, I collected all my meds and threw them down the toilet.

I was sure this new drug would defeat my depression at last. I would regret that decision for the next six months.

Before then, I had never experienced medication withdrawal. In fact, I had never varied the instructions prescribed by my doctor and had never stopped using a drug on my own. Every psych drug has its own *half-life*, meaning it stays in your system for a few days after it has been discontinued. For the first week following my medication change, I felt the same as before. On the eighth night, that changed. I was sleeping when suddenly my body went haywire. I couldn't control anything. My nerves were on fire, as if I were being dipped into a vat of scalding water. I woke Lenni and had her hold me while I cried uncontrollably.

The withdrawal passed in a couple of days, but the storm created with the medication change continued for five agonizing months. My new shrink advised me to give the drug time—the results would be well worth it he insured me. Each day, I waited for the drug to take effect. Meanwhile, I was still out of control. It acted as a stimulant, so I was constantly revved up. My blood pressure soared. I had to be on-the-go all the time. I couldn't relax enough to do normal tasks, making work impossible, and constructive decision-making was out of the question. For example, I impulsively decided to revitalize the store with a complete remodel, costing over $100,000. Not having the money, I borrowed it, plunging me further into debt.

Sleep eluded me. I would doze off for an hour or two, abruptly wake up, then go downstairs, and listen to music till dawn. I was in such bad shape that I had to miss Cari's national gymnastics meet in Niagara Falls, New York. She earned first place on the balance beam as a twelve-year-old, competing against girls who were fifteen. It was a big deal, and I missed it because I couldn't slow myself down.

I was unaware that the agitation, restlessness, and impulsivity were all symptoms caused by Desyrel, the miracle drug the new psychiatrist had prescribed. In addition, I felt more depressed than ever. I finally called Harding Hospital, told them I wanted to be admitted, and arrived at midnight. The staff was waiting for me at the admission desk. After an hour-long therapy session, I was told that

Dr. Head wanted me to return the next afternoon for a three o'clock appointment.

The next day, Lenni took me to a nearby park to calm down before the appointment. We began walking on the path when my legs just quit working. It was as if they were encased in cement. The harder I tried to walk, the more impossible it became. Lenni slowly helped me get to the car, and we immediately headed for Harding.

The first thing Dr. Head said when he saw me was, "What the hell happened to you? You were doing so well. Why did you change medications?"

Sheepishly, I told him about seeing the other psychiatrist in his absence and his advice for me to change medication. When I divulged who the doctor was, he, perhaps unprofessionally, told me that the same doctor had worked at Harding Hospital but had been dismissed.

Turning his attention to my dilemma, he wrote prescriptions for Lithium, Navane, and Inderal, a beta-blocker that would control my racing heart. By the end of the week, I not only began to feel better but also more in control. Doctor Head wanted to try a new drug for the severe ruminations, but without hesitation, I told him I was not willing to try another new psychiatric drug. However, I felt I was able turn my attention to work and deal with all the problems associated with it.

CHAPTER 31

Goodbye Wilson's, Hello S. W.

Two new upscale shopping malls, each with a variety of fine men's and women's clothing, had just opened in Columbus. They cut into my business dramatically. Then, without warning, two of my top salespeople quit and went to work for my competitors. Thirty percent of my business evaporated overnight. It was another huge blow that forced me to borrow more money just to stay afloat.

By the end of 1994, the store was $250,000 in debt with zero chance of turning things around, and mentally and physically, I was a wreck. The store had hit rock bottom. I had no option but to liquidate. A going-out-of-business sale could produce the needed cash to pay my creditors if done correctly. Fortunately, we had a great relationship with our buying office in New York City. They gave me the name of a well-respected company that specialized in running store closings. On January 10, 1995, I signed the contract that would lead to the closing of Wilson's.

Immediately, I began working with the liquidating company's representative. We prepared for a sale that would last three months. The shelves and racks were stocked with fresh merchandise (provided by the company running the sale because I couldn't afford to purchase it). I put my faith in this rep, crossed my fingers, and on March 9, the going out of business sale began.

Any apprehension, I had disappeared as the sale proved to be a great success. In less than three months, all the debt was paid, and I even ended up with a little extra cash. May 27 marked the close of my fourth-generation clothing store. As I walked out the back door for the final time, I looked back, smiled, and gave it the finger.

I felt as though the weight of the world had been lifted from my shoulders. No longer did I have to fight every day for something that was beating me up. I was finally free from that tremendous burden.

Ready for the next challenge, I knew I couldn't work for someone else, but I did put my twenty-five years of clothing experience to work. After talking with people already in the custom clothing business and visiting manufacturers, I opened my new custom clothing business selling directly to customers throughout Ohio. I called it S. W. Wilson, Personal Clothier. I took hundreds of fabric swatches to a client's home or office, took their measurements, helped the client choose any design features they wanted, and then sent the information to manufacturers who made the clothing specifically designed for that client.

From the beginning, S. W. was a success. The first year I sold almost $200,000 worth of merchandise, making more than I did the last couple of years at Wilson's.

Earlier in her work life, Lenni had worked at the Columbus Zoo. She had been responsible for designing and erecting the zoo's outdoor displays, including hanging thousands of Christmas lights. Since 1990, Lenni had been working for me at Wilson's. She handled all the computer work. It was natural for her to continue working for me as I began my new venture. It was her job to take care of everything I didn't handle.

One day, my impulsivity came roaring back when I heard a friend of mine say he didn't think I would do well with my clothing business. I pondered this and, overnight, decided I would do better working in real estate because I had been managing the family real estate holdings for years. So, like an idiot, I gave into my disorder, got my realtor's license, and tried my hand at commercial real estate. At the same time, I shut down my clothing business. Once again, I let my fear of failure force me into a radical move—all because someone with no knowledge of my business made a derogatory remark. It proved to be another in a long list of debacles.

I selected the real estate company that did most of the commercial business in Delaware to work for. However, that association lasted only two years because the broker, who was the owner of the company, cheated me out of several lucrative deals. For the next year or so, I stumbled from one real estate company to another with little success. Even though I was strict about taking my medication, depression continued to overwhelm me. Then, unexpectedly, I received a phone call that put me back on the right path.

The call was from a man who was a private custom clothier from Columbus, and he offered to sell me his customer list since he was moving out of state. Right away, I jumped at the chance. We made a deal, and I started S. W. Wilson, Personal Clothier again. Along with my original set of customers and his, I was ready to begin anew. I was doing what I enjoyed, being my own boss and setting my own schedule. That proved to be very important when our family was hit with a new crisis in 1998.

CHAPTER 32

Mom, They Think I Have Cancer

It was a Friday afternoon in late August when Lenni received a call while working at the Columbus Zoo. She couldn't detect which of our three girls was calling because of the sobbing on the other end of the line. She finally realized it was Jami, our eldest daughter.

"Mom! They think I have cancer!"

Lenni immediately left work and drove to the high school tennis courts where Jami was coaching the girls' team. Together they went into the school, found a quiet spot in the hallway, sat down on the floor, and tried not to cry.

Jami had received a chest x-ray, taken for a lingering cough, and a small lump was discovered near her collarbone. Our family doctor suspected it may be lymphoma and wanted a biopsy done. He didn't pull any punches but succeeded in scaring the hell out of our twenty-three-year-old daughter.

Lenni calmed Jami down just enough so that she could finish coaching the tennis team and then immediately headed home to share the news with me. Once I digested the news, I called a customer of mine who happened to be a well-known surgeon in Marion, a small town north of Delaware. I asked him if he would perform the biopsy, and he agreed. He scheduled it for September the second.

To complicate matters, that was the same day Ohio State was to hold its graduation ceremony for our middle daughter, Cari. How could we be in Columbus and Marion at the same time? We didn't want to disappoint Cari, yet Jami's life was at stake.

After sharing the news with our close friend and neighbor, we worked out a solution. We would take Jami up to Marion, get her ready for surgery, and then our neighbor (who was practically a second mom to Jami) would take a personal day from teaching and stay with Jami until she came out of surgery. We all felt comfortable with this plan. Meanwhile, we would race down to Columbus to attend Cari's graduation.

Our thoughts were on Jami throughout the ceremony, and we could hardly wait to get back to the hospital to speak with the surgeon. Jami was in recovery as the surgeon came out to address Lenni and me. The news was not good.

He discovered the primary source of the lump on her collarbone was a 5 cm mass behind her sternum. We had to wait for lab results, but he was certain that it was non-Hodgkin's lymphoma, a sometimes treatable, but not curable blood cancer. We hugged each other and cried while I sat in shock, trying to absorb the news.

Upon the surgeon's recommendation, we took Jami to the James Cancer Hospital at Ohio State University. She had a bone marrow aspiration to see if the cancer had spread. Fortunately, it had not. It was the first of many, many tests she would have to endure.

Jami had married her high school sweetheart the year before. He was a nice guy about six foot three and three hundred pounds. However, he was extremely lazy. Even after Jami's cancer diagnosis, he did very little to help at home. On a couple occasions, he and his buddies drank beer on the porch, while Jami mowed the lawn. Then, it got worse. He ballooned to four hundred forty pounds and had to stay in a special bed in the basement, surrounded by chips, cookies, and soda cans. One day, he had to be removed from the basement to go to the hospital. It took four paramedics to lift him from the bed and put him on a gurney. While they were carrying him away, he dropped from their grasp and fell to the floor. Instead of staying calm, he screamed, "I'm going to sue!" It took all Jami's strength not to give up on him at that moment.

I arranged my schedule so that I could spend as much time as possible with Jami, supporting her throughout chemotherapy regimens, radiation, and even an autologous bone marrow transplant using her own stem cells. Jami's husband was a burden during her first hospitalization, so she made up her mind to divorce him. Finally, he was out of her life, but there was a stipulation. Jami had to turn over her savings to him even though she had supported him for over a year. At least he was gone.

All along, I had been keeping my close friend David aware of how Jami was doing. His reaction to her condition and finalized divorce was to fly her and her best friend, Tara, along with Lenni and me, to Las Vegas for a night in the casinos and then on to Los Angeles, where David hired a limousine to take Jami and Tara on a sightseeing excursion. He also arranged for Jami and Tara to appear as *extras* on Becker.

Despite the initial success of the treatments, the tumor stopped shrinking. It was clear that Jami needed a second transplant, this time from a donor. Her chances of survival were extremely low, but we all decided it was worth a shot rather than watching her grow weak as she waited to die.

A donor was found, and the transplant took place on June 27. Ironically, that was Lenni's fiftieth birthday. There would be no celebration. All we could do was hope for the best. Unfortunately, Jami's condition deteriorated. She was placed on a ventilator, but her organs were shutting down. She passed away on August 2, 2000. It was the absolute worst day of my life.

Jami's passing had an amazing effect upon our family. Instead of falling into despair, we became closer than ever. During the almost two years that Jami had been sick, our daughter Cari gave birth to her two girls, Mia and Avery, who brought us much-needed joy. Casi, our youngest daughter, had received permission from Arizona State to miss the beginning days of college to stay home with Jami and us. Once Jami passed, we packed up our cars and, together with Casi's boyfriend, Ryan, began the long journey from Ohio to Arizona to get them to ASU. She and Ryan then flew home three weeks later for Jami's memorial service.

As for Lenni and me, we spent two nights in Santa Fe, New Mexico, on our way home from dropping off Casi at school. Away from the many friends who supported us throughout Jami's illness, we welcomed the solitude, but the loss of our girl was made real for the first time. We held each other, cried, and realized that our strength as best friends would get us through this horrible time. Our bond was stronger than ever.

CHAPTER 33

Teenage Depression

My three daughters had experienced mental illness in some form. As a teenager, Jami fell into her own depression. Luckily, we knew a wonderful child psychologist who guided her through some tough times. Naturally, I felt responsible. Doctor Head and I had once discussed the likelihood of passing depression and other mental illness from one generation to another. He acknowledged that in his thirty years of experience, he was positive there was a genetic relationship to why people suffered from mental illness.

In addition to Jami, our other daughters Cari and Casi had experienced similar bouts of mental illness. Cari's symptoms were like mine: rumination out of control, fear of impending disaster, and some OCD. Following the birth of her first child, she fell victim to postpartum blues that ravaged her for weeks. Casi's problem was anger. At the drop of a hat, she would fly out of control. Luckily, all three of the girls were helped by proper medication and counseling.

Along with our family's own bouts with mental illness, there were two other terrible teenage tragedies that led me to enlighten others about the tremendous stress our children were dealing with.

Every year during the Christmas season, I would hire two or three high school girls to wrap packages at the store. One year I hired Angie, a sophomore at one of the county high schools. She was energetic, bubbly, and did most anything she was asked to do with a smile. Early one Saturday morning, her best friend, who also worked for me, came into the store crying profusely. She told me Angie had shot and killed herself the night before. I never heard why.

She was the second young person I knew who had committed suicide. Years before, the son of one of my college buddies shot himself right in front of his parents. He had just been released from police custody for breaking and entering. My friend told me his son hadn't been himself for quite a while. These two senseless deaths, along with our own family issues, helped me see that teenage and young adult mental problems were a huge issue that people failed to recognize. So I began addressing high school psychology classes in Delaware County. What I discovered was unnerving.

Many kids were struggling mentally, and no one, not teachers, counselors, or parents, was aware of the extent to which these kids struggled. In fact, one health teacher got upset with me when I asked her how often she talked with her students about mental health. She said, "Once in the fall and once in the spring."

"Is that often enough?" I countered.

"Well. We don't want to scare them," she offered and walked away unwilling to admit she was part of the problem.

At the end of each presentation, I asked anyone who was struggling to meet with me in private. To my surprise, one of the most popular and brightest students at one school showed up. She told me she couldn't take the pressure she was under each day to get all A's, ace the SAT exams, and get accepted into one of the top universities. She admitted to occasionally cutting herself with a sharp object, a common practice among those suffering from a feeling of despair, known as *cutting*. Cutting is done to relieve the overwhelming stress and emptiness of their lives. I assured her help was available. I suggested she seek out a professional therapist who could help her, and I gave her the name of the child psychologist who had helped Jami. She promised she would and walked away with tears in her eyes.

A second young lady showed up with a totally different reason for being depressed. She said she had no friends, was extremely lonely, and hated school, and her parents didn't understand her. All she wanted to do was quit and run away. That was a scenario I heard constantly. I gave her the same advice as I did the other young lady. But why was no adult aware of what was going on in their own schools? Were they that oblivious?

The fact is, no student is immune from the torture of mental stress and depression. Because of the stigma attached to this illness, most children won't admit to what they are going through, but there are definite signs they are in trouble: grades plummeting, sleeplessness, low self-esteem, and lack of energy. I wasn't immune to what I heard from the students. All of it brought back vivid memories of what I had gone through. Even though my meds helped tremendously, I was drawn into a feeling of helplessness as related to what the young people shared.

CHAPTER 34

Dr. Warner

Doctor Head had died a few years earlier, so I sought out a new psychiatrist in 2002. Doctor John Warner had a private practice about thirty miles north of Delaware. We met in an old TB hospital that had been transformed into a mental hospital. I told him about my constant ruminating about anything and anyone. He prescribed Paxil—the same new drug Dr. Head had recommended to me years ago that I had refused to take. This time, I relented.

Within two weeks, the racing thoughts subsided so much that I started feeling as if the addition of Paxil was the missing link to finding the correct combination of drugs that would work best for me. My new *cocktail* marked the beginning of an improved life for me. Most of the horrible thinking went away. It was as if I was in control of my mind for the first time in forty years.

Doctor Warner and I met every three months to renew my medication and to discuss how I was doing. This regimen continued until about 2006, when I met with him for an appointment. Before he arrived, I was looking out the window when he drove up. Immediately, he got out of the car, ran to the back, removed something from the trunk, dropped it, and then kicked it down the driveway. A few minutes later, he came into his office where I was seated, said hello, and began washing the office door. Next, he began eating what looked like oatmeal the whole time we were talking. Then he asked me if I could help him get a job with a psychologist in Delaware. It seemed he had been making a lot of money when the

TB clinic had been open, but since it closed, his practice was not doing well.

I was stunned, but my first observation was that he wasn't coping with it well. The first thing I did after our session was to alert his nurse. She acknowledged that he was in bad shape. After calling the mental health department, we called a therapist friend of his. Unfortunately, before the therapist arrived, a police car showed up, probably alerted by the mental health department. The police met with Dr. Warner in his office, while the staff, the therapist who had just arrived, and I huddled outside. Then, Dr. Warner appeared at the open window yelling, "I am not going to commit suicide!" With nothing more to do, I got in my car and returned home.

The next day, Dr. Warner's practice was closed. This was unnerving to me, as I depended on Dr. Warner to keep me on an even keel. However, upon reflecting upon where I was in my life, I realized if my personal care physician agreed to prescribe my medications, I would persevere without a psychiatrist or therapist. This proved to be the right decision, as I didn't seek psychiatric help until I saw Dr. Amy Bjorkman in 2020. And that was just to find answers to my traumas. For the first time in many, many years, I felt I could control my mental health myself.

I never found out what Dr. Warner's diagnosis was, but I read in the paper that he died in 2012. He had never reopened his practice.

CHAPTER 35

Authority Figures

One day in 2002, while I was working with a client in Dayton, Ohio, he told me about a fantastic new custom clothing company that had just been established in Columbus. It was expected to change the way custom clothing was sold in the United States.

Morgan, a young, brash, know-it-all, had set up a contract with a small custom clothing manufacturer in Hong Kong to produce quality clothing at substantially less cost. I decided to check it out and gave him a call. I met with him at his showroom the next day.

We went over his business plan, which outlined a strategy to have salespeople selling his product throughout the country. Because of his family's many connections, he had been able to sell over a million dollars' worth of clothing his first year and had hundreds of potential clients yet to contact. His idea of assembling a large team of professional clothiers to travel the country selling high-quality clothing made in Hong Kong was brilliant. However, there were a few problems. He showed me racks of client's clothing that had been returned for a refund because they didn't fit or were poor quality. It was apparent all his profits had been lost. While inspecting the clothing, I could see that the construction was poor and needed to be upgraded, or a new manufacturer should be found. He promised to fix the quality issue. Finding the rest of the business plan sound, I gave him a dollar to solidify our deal to work together.

From then on, he called me nightly to discuss the business. It was clear that Morgan thought of me as a partner rather than an employee. Sometimes we talked for over an hour, but no matter how

I tried to persuade him, he wouldn't change manufacturers. Because he was selling a lot of clothing, he thought business was great. It seemed that his clients thought so highly of his family, they were willing to continue purchasing poor-quality clothing that took way too long to be delivered. To my amazement, the sales and profits grew, so additional salespeople were hired.

My clients expected high-quality clothing delivered in approximately five weeks. My boss's clothing took at least eight weeks for clients to receive it. I began losing my own customers and a lot of money. They didn't care if the clothing was cheaper. They expected what I had always given them: quality clothing, priced fairly, and delivered on time. I was in a horrible predicament and had no idea what to do. Instead of standing up for my beliefs and demanding better products, even if they were more expensive, I very aggressively told Morgan he was ruining his company because he sold inferior clothing to unsuspecting clients. Then, just as I always did, I quit. My inability to deal with Morgan put me in a precarious position: no job and no prospect of one. To make matters worse, a few years later, after expanding the business throughout the country, Morgan sold the business for several million dollars.

When I was still working for Morgan, he asked me to establish our own wholesale custom clothing division. For a few months, I traveled throughout the United States visiting personal clothiers like myself, enticing them with our products. The venture didn't work out, but I struck up relationships with several custom clothiers. Upon hearing I had quit my position, one of them in Florida knew of a Hong Kong manufacturer looking for a United States sales representative. After an initial phone interview with the patriarchal owner, he flew me to Hong Kong to meet with his two sons, who were part owners of the company. They were impressed with my background and experience and offered me the position right after I returned to Delaware.

Working for this company proved to be the perfect job for me. I traveled the United States with all expenses paid, made excellent money, and loved every minute of it. During 2007, my first year with them, I established a hundred new accounts.

Then, in 2008, the world's economy fell off a cliff. The Great Recession created a state of financial collapse. Almost every business was affected, including this one. The owners blamed me for the downturn in active accounts. I started suggesting it was their fault because they weren't providing proper customer service. Once again, I began acting as if I was in charge and implying they should defer to me. Their response was to cut my salary by 20 percent. That marked the beginning of several turbulent years for me at the company, all because I couldn't control my response to a tough situation. Finally, in 2013, I was fired. The only option was to recreate S. W. Wilson, Personal Clothier this time in Phoenix where we had lived since 2008 to be with our family.

My business prospered, although not as well as in Ohio. I enjoyed the freedom it provided, and I didn't have to answer to anyone. The problem was the customers were different than those in Ohio. Instead of selling suits from $800 to $2,000, my new clientele demanded even better quality and at a much higher price. It became normal to sell suits from $3,000 to $6,000 and shirts between $300 and $700. This created an environment I was not prepared for. My clients demanded perfection, and with that, my stress levels flew off the charts. It was impossible for me to please some of them.

I started getting more and more returns, and, usually, I was not given the chance to correct them. Not only did I begin losing money, but I also started arguing with some clients and sending them nasty emails. A couple of times I stormed out of appointments because the customer was being unreasonable. Never, in all my years in the clothing business, had I acted that way. I was not myself. It was unnerving, scary, and I needed a change.

More than anything, I wanted to represent and travel for a clothing manufacturer again, so I contacted a new manufacturer to inquire about possible open sales territories. To my surprise, the West Coast area was available. Following a couple of interviews, I accepted an offer.

The owner of the new company agreed to allow me to continue selling clothing to my preferred clients in the Phoenix and Tucson markets. One day, my boss called to inform me another clothing retailer I had called on in Tucson on behalf of the wholesale company demanded I stop selling to my own customers in his town. He wanted me to turn them over to him, or he wouldn't purchase any more clothing from us. Infuriated, my boss told me in no uncertain terms to discontinue selling on my own. I should have agreed to close it down, but, as always, I retaliated, started yelling at my boss, and quit. Once again, I had hurt only myself. I had been unable to control my irrational impulse to strike out at the man in charge.

It was clear that bipolar disorder can raise its ugly head in many ways. The problem was my mental issues prevented me from succeeding. Even though I had never considered the possibility, I realized my rape experience might be a factor in my impulsiveness. Did anyone who threatened me send me into *fight or flight* mode? I would investigate the possibility soon.

CHAPTER 36

Dr. Bjorkman

In 2008, just five years after building our dream house outside Delaware, Lenni and I were faced with a huge decision. Cari and her husband, Mike, moved their family to Phoenix, Arizona. Mike was embarking on a new career, and we wanted to be a part of their lives and those of our grandchildren, Mia and Avery. We had frequented the state every five years or so since getting married, and it didn't take much to convince us to make the move. Who wouldn't want to wake up to sunshine almost every day of the year? So we sold our beloved home and headed west. No more gloomy Ohio days for us.

I was still working for the Hong Kong company at the time, and everything seemed to fall into place. We were in our own world with our family in our favorite part of the country.

Much to our delight, Casi and Ryan, along with Rosco the boxer and Hercules the gecko, moved from Florida to Phoenix the following year. I continued as a sales representative until I was let go and returned to selling custom clothing directly to new clients in Arizona, and then finally in September of 2019, I retired. With extra time on my hands, I took up the task of facing the traumas that had led to my severe depression and sought out relief from the symptoms that still plagued me.

I found Dr. Amy Bjorkman during a search for leading trauma psychologists in the Phoenix area. She had an extensive background in helping patients deal with psychological issues that had engulfed them throughout their lives. As for me, I wanted her to help me understand three specific incidents, the first of which was my rape.

Did it cause my bipolar disorder? Did it cause my fear of sexual relationships? Did it cause my reactions to authority figures?

Doctor Bjorkman and I delved into my childhood, starting with my earliest memories. It was clear I was well-nurtured and loved as a young child. However, as my father became less and less attentive to me and my siblings, and my mother had to deal with her own demons, including tic douloureux. I no longer received the attention I desired. I felt so abandoned and alone that I couldn't reveal to them what had happened to me in the theater. I was forced to deal with it on my own, which meant not dealing with it at all.

The more Dr. Bjorkman and I discussed my rape, the more we agreed that it did influence my bipolar tendencies; however, there were other factors too. The question of whether any of my ancestors were mentally ill was a possibility. When I did some research, I discovered that one of my mother's ancestors hanged himself in a barn, and another, known as *Crazy Mary*, was confined to a mental institution for the last twenty years of her life. Perhaps I had inherited their tendencies, and that, coupled with the rape, was partly responsible for my bipolar disorder. Doctor Head had told me from the beginning that I had a chemical imbalance in my brain that caused mental anguish. Doctor Bjorkman confirmed she believed it, and so did many of her colleagues.

The second major incident I wanted to discuss was dealing with the night my ex-girlfriend showed up at the Rollins sorority party in 1970. At the time, I thought I was still in love with her and had hoped to rekindle our relationship when I saw her. It was not to be. I always believed that incident had triggered my severe depression, but there was something else too. I remembered how Sherry had dressed as if to disguise her figure. At the time, I couldn't figure it out.

Even as I gained more control over my depression, I didn't think about her very often over the next forty years until one day I came across her name and email on our college alumni website. I was still curious as to why she had looked as she did at the spring party. On a whim, I decided to contact her. Right away, she wrote back, and we exchanged emails, catching up on each other's lives.

In one email, I asked her why she had come to the sorority party and why she had left so soon after seeing me. She blatantly lied, saying she didn't remember seeing me. Her lie, plus not wanting to use protection during sex, and the way she appeared at that Kappa party made me think there may have been another reason why she left the party so abruptly. Could it be that she had been pregnant with my child?

I continued to bug her, bombarding her with emails. Determined to discover the truth. As I was going to Ohio soon, I asked her to meet me. At first, she agreed but then cancelled without explanation, telling me not to contact her again. I couldn't understand why. Reluctantly, I asked Dr. Bjorkman to help me figure out how to proceed.

Doctor Bjorkman's method was never to directly advise but to guide me through the process of making my own decision. Following weeks of debate, I sent an email to Connie in which I asked her point blank if she had been pregnant with my child. Her answer, "Are you kidding me? No way!"

I asked her why she had returned so quickly to her old boyfriend and if she had planned to be with him all along. Was I just a fling? She never answered, confirming what I had expected: I was nothing more than a way for her to pass the time. My quest was over. Finally, I had the closure I so desperately needed.

Perhaps I had been irrational in pursuing this question, but being overcome with bipolar disorder made it impossible for me to let the issue go until it was resolved.

The third incident centered around how to deal with a side effect I had from one of my psychiatric drugs. In 2003, my doctor detected a rise in my creatinine level after a routine blood tests. I was referred to a nephrologist who determined my kidney function had fallen to 55 percent. The culprit? Lithium. It was no surprise to me, as I always knew it was possible, and the benefit I received using Lithium was worth it. No side effect was bad enough to discontinue the drug and possibly slip back into massive depression.

The kidney damage worsened over the years, until my kidney function had fallen to 14 percent by 2020. I needed a kidney transplant. But in 2018, a blood test showed I had developed a cancer in the blood known as Waldenstrom lymphoma, which was extremely rare. This really freaked me out, as there was no cure, and my life expectancy was five to eight years. Two transplant hospitals told me I wasn't qualified for a transplant because of the cancer. What was happening to me? Not only did I have a serious kidney problem but also cancer. My first choice for a hospital to do the transplant was Mayo Clinic in Phoenix, and the two which turned me down were secondary. Following a week of intensive testing at Mayo, they agreed to do the transplant. However, there was a hitch. The average wait to find a deceased donor is three to five years, so a live donor was preferable. Four wonderful people agreed to be donors. Unfortunately, one at a time, they were dismissed as possible donors for various reasons because of Mayo's strict transplant protocol. To make matters worse, my blood type was O-, a difficult type to match, even with a deceased donor. In August 2020, with my kidney function still deteriorating, it was time to consider going on dialysis.

I was struggling with the concept of dialysis. Would it be worth it? Would a donor be found? Should I just allow my kidneys to eventually fail and pass away?

It was time to head back to talk to Dr. Bjorkman. She and I discussed my options and feelings. Obviously, it was my decision, but she really helped me put things in perspective. I decided to give dialysis a try, knowing I could stop if it became too demanding or uncomfortable.

In September of 2020, I began peritoneal dialysis. I had a catheter implanted through my stomach into my peritoneum. While we waited until the incisions healed before beginning the treatment, Lenni and I took classes to learn how to do the necessary daily regimen. Once a day, I manually filled my stomach with 2000mm of solution, *dwelled* for four hours, and then drained out the solution— all in the comfort of my home. If it becomes necessary to fill more than once a day, I could either do it during the night using a machine or decide to go to a dialysis center several times a week for four hours at a time. Doing it at home is preferable, as I have the freedom to move around and leave the house while I dwell, rather than be confined to a chair with an IV for several hours.

For now, my spirits are high. Besides, I've been through a lot worse than this in my life. There is nothing worse than losing a child or anything more frightening than suicidal thoughts caused by unchecked depression.

CHAPTER 37

Group

Spirituality often comes into play when dealing with bipolar disorder. Does it help? It seems to be about a fifty-fifty split between those who think it does and those who don't. I am in the group that thinks it doesn't help, even though when I was in my teens I believed in Jesus. In fact, when I saw the movie *Rosemary's Baby* in 1968, I was appalled by the way they portrayed the power of the devil.

For the last six years, I have been facilitating two mental health groups in Phoenix. Many of my group members have turned to a higher power, using their faith to get relief from their mental anguish. At times in group, we talk about religion and faith and the effect they have on bipolar disorder and whether it is beneficial to forgive our abuser(s). For some, the answer is yes, and they say that it has brought them some peace of mind and lessened their burden. Others emphatically say they will never forgive. Personally, I have always been opposed to the thought of forgiveness because I feel it gives too much power to the assailant.

In the early 1970s, while in the worst of my depression, I turned to God for help. Each night I went to the Bible, asked him for help, and read aloud Psalm 23. I implored him to help me deal with my condition, but nothing happened. I received no advice on how to deal with my hopelessness. It became clear to me that there was no deity who would help with the world's problems or mine. I realized then that I was an atheist.

When we moved to Phoenix in 2008, I had a strong desire to speak to high school students once again about teenage mental illness. However, schools preferred peers to address classes. That meant that anyone over thirty-five did not qualify. Undeterred, I continued to seek various means of getting involved with people crushed by mental illness. I attempted to work with a couple of national organizations but found them too restrictive, especially when it came to telling my own story. They thought it was too much of a trigger and wanted me to water it down. I was not willing to tell a different version of my life just to please them.

One day, I saw a request in a local newspaper for a facilitator to take over a mental health support group. I answered the ad, was accepted, and went through several hours of training. In the summer of 2015, I took over my first group. A year later, I added a second group. It had been an exciting and rewarding experience working with people ages eighteen to seventy-five. They came from various backgrounds, but all shared the struggles of mental illness.

During the six years I've been facilitating, I had worked with more than a thousand individuals suffering from mental illness. What I have learned is that a high percentage of them had been physically or sexually abused. Most of the time, the cruelty came when they were young and vulnerable or through personal tragedy. One person informed the group that his father had tied him to a post in their basement and burned his body with cigarettes. Another shared that his wife had given birth to a baby boy, only to discover the baby dead in his crib just a few days later. The couple was devastated, and his wife was so distraught that she went into the garage, shut the door, got in the car, and turned on the ignition.

Upon returning home from work, he found her, but it was too late. The trauma so overwhelmed him that each night at bedtime, he sit in the closet with a baseball bat, waiting for whoever is coming to get him. One girl went on a first date with a boy she just met. He took her to a nearby park and raped her. Like me, she never told anyone for years what had happened to her. She just bottled it up inside herself. It was not until many years of therapy and medication that she was able to verbalize her experience. Many others were in total fear of their parents or relatives who forced them into sexual situations, constantly berated them, or beat them.

Having endured sexual abuse myself, I felt a kinship with these individuals. We understood one another, unlike those who have not suffered in this way. Most of these individuals could open up to the group, even if only slightly. I believed it is because they find themselves in a setting with people who have gone through situations like their own. Still, there continues to be tragedy.

A few years ago, one of my clothing customers went to a park and shot himself. He had gotten into financial trouble and probably saw no other way out. Shortly after that, a friend of mine, who was a pillar of the community and loved by everyone, hanged himself in his basement. He had been going through extensive therapy, but I don't know if he was medicated. Only his wife knew he had suffered from deep depression for years. They hid it so well that no one suspected what he was going through.

Unfortunately, he couldn't cope any longer. I went to his memorial service, where one of his close friends expressed that he was pissed that the man who killed himself could do this to his friends. I was astounded that he didn't consider the victim's state of mind. This showed the total ignorance the public has about mental illness. I spoke up and told the gathering that he didn't do it to spite them, he did it because he no longer wanted to live his life in so much distress, and he probably thought it was best for everyone.

Two of my group members have also committed suicide. One was a lady of about fifty who sought relief from her mental anguish by injecting herself with a lethal amount of her insulin. The other member was an intelligent graduate school student, a young lady who only came to the group three times. She told us she had suicidal ideations but wouldn't take her life because she and her mother had a great relationship, and she didn't want to cause her mother any pain. Evidently, even that wasn't enough. She took her life the next week.

I have suffered from type II bipolar disorder for over fifty years. It has been a roller-coaster ride of deep depression followed by periods of normalcy. I have gone through months of great happiness, then fallen off a cliff, and back into the deep depression.

Although I suffer from mental illness, I consider myself lucky. With great doctors (for the most part) and tremendous advancements in medications, I have been able to cope with my illness and lead a relatively normal life, especially since receiving Lithium. I have also been fortunate to have had a tremendous support system from my family and friends. Anyone who deals with a person suffering from mental illness must learn to be patient and empathetic, not judgmental.

I must admit I'm not totally free of my mental problems. I still make irrational decisions, worry about past mistakes, and dwell on the *what-ifs*. I have high blood pressure and am extremely impatient, even though I am properly medicated and have gone through extensive therapy. Even so, all things considered, I am doing well.

Many others are not as fortunate. With few financial resources, many are unable to find or unable to afford professional help and medication. With the way insurance companies have undercut provisions for mental health coverage, even if a person has coverage, psychiatrists and psychologists refuse to take insurance payments. Then there are an unknown number of suffering people who don't seek any type of relief other than alcohol or illicit drugs.

For those who are below a certain income level or are unable to work, the state of Arizona offers the Arizona Health Care Cost Containment System, a part of the Medicaid system. Having investigated AHCCCS a bit, I believe it is a good program but still inadequate in many ways. The waiting time to see a therapist can be three months or more. When the patient does finally get in to see a therapist, they may find that, because the turnover is so great, their therapist is no longer with the program when their next appointment is scheduled. Thus, a real lack of continuity. The agency is also prohibited from prescribing various new or expensive medications, preventing patients from receiving the most current treatments. The biggest problem is that AHCCCS just can't keep up with the vast number of people who need their services.

Recently, I learned that no matter how great the medications may be, less than 50 percent of patients respond favorably at first, and it sometimes takes years to get the combination of drugs to work effectively. Their days continue to be filled with anxiety, fear, sleepless nights, and the feeling that their lives are meaningless. Sometimes, when they are manic, they are so supercharged that they come close to ruining their lives financially and alienate all those in their life.

My hope is that those suffering will recognize that help is out there. It may be uncomfortable and it may take more than a few tries to find what works for them, but they must persevere to gain control over their demons. Countless times I have seen firsthand where a person overwhelmed with depression or mania has been able to put their lives back together by constantly rebooting their medication regime when necessary and through vigilant therapy. Bipolar disorder, although not curable, can be treated, allowing the afflicted to live productive, enjoyable lives.

As for me, I am seventy-three years old. During my life, I have lived through the hell of severe depression, which made me want to escape life by my own hand. But there has also been an abundance of joy which I wouldn't have wanted to miss, and that has made everything worthwhile.

EPILOGUE

My family and I have endured countless tragedies. Not only have I had to deal with my bipolar disorder. My daughter Jami died at a young age. Lenni had to have a double mastectomy, and I had prostate cancer and had to have my prostate removed. Plus, there is my kidney disease. Throughout all of this, I have remained a steadfast atheist.

Last September, Cari convinced me to get a second opinion about my cancer. I agreed and made an appointment with the Mayo Clinic in Phoenix. As I walked into the conference room, the doctor informed me that I did not have Waldenstrom lymphoma. What I have is a form of precancer, and I only need to have it checked out every six months. It would not interfere with a transplant. That's number one.

Three weeks later, while at a diner I frequent daily, a waitress came up to me and offered to donate her kidney to me. She filled out all the necessary paperwork and sent it to Mayo. She was not a match, but we could try for an exchange of kidneys between other recipients. This process would take up to a year. For the first time in a long time, I had hope. That's number two.

Then, on December 4, 2021, I received an early morning call from Mayo. A twenty- or thirty-year-old had passed away the night before, and his kidney was a close match to mine, so they wanted to do my transplant the next day. That's number three.

As I write this, it has been four weeks since my transplant. I was told there could be a variety of temporary side effects. The one I hadn't anticipated was hallucinations. I began seeing lots of people, many from my past. When I would reach out for them, they vanished into thin air. Other times I tried to talk to them, only to get no response. Fortunately, the hallucinations only lasted two days. Then there was the tinnitus or ringing in my ears. The sound reminded me of mosquitos. That too subsided. Cramping in my hands and legs has been a problem that I'm still dealing with. Despite this, right now I feel better than I have in many years.

I have spent the time going back to Mayo for several blood tests and other checkups. I take approximately thirty pills per day, twenty in the morning and ten at night, always at eight o'clock because they must be taken twelve hours apart. Although I still get tired, my fatigue which previously prevented me from doing even simple housework has disappeared. My doctors tell me the kidney is a good match for me and should last about nine years.

The other day, I told Lenni the chain of events that led to my transplant was incredible. Everything just fell into place. I found out I didn't have cancer. I was offered a kidney, and out of the blue, I received the transplant I thought was at least a year away. It made me think about what else had occurred in my life that was out of the ordinary and couldn't be explained.

Immediately, the memory of the football bowl game came to mind. It had taken place in the same city in which Lenni was going to spend Thanksgiving break. Meeting her there ultimately led to us getting back together. Next August, we'll celebrate out fiftieth anniversary. Coincidence? That's number four.

Then, I remembered the time I was swimming laps at the Y when a paraplegic man rolled up to the side of the pool in a wheelchair. He slid into the water and began swimming. As I watched him, I noticed that because his legs sank in the water, he had to struggle mightily to swim. When he finished his second lap, I stopped him and suggested he use a float to hold up his legs, making it easier to swim. It was about eight o'clock in the evening, no one else was around, and all swim equipment had been put away. Nothing was available. Then, out of the corner of my eye, I saw something close to a wall. When I went to investigate, I saw it was a float with a strap around it. Perfect for what he needed. When I attached it to his leg, he was able to hold them on top of the water, and his swimming became less labored. As I resumed my swimming, I couldn't stop wondering how the one thing, the only thing that would work, was left on the floor? Number five.

For the past month, I have been pondering this strange course of events. I have even considered the possibility that there is something out there watching over us. It is a concept too implausible for me to fully comprehend, but it has undoubtedly changed my thinking. I am shedding my stance on religion and now consider myself an agnostic. I don't believe in God, but I acknowledge there is the possibility he exists.

Having experienced a lifetime of mental issues and spent many hours working with those afflicted, I have concluded there are millions of people who suffer with their own demons but never seek or receive quality professional help. They go through each day alone and bewildered by what's happening to them. Our world is always in turmoil, and when you add the ways in which people can physically, mentally, and sexually harm one another, it is no wonder our cities are overwhelmed with the homeless and mentally ill who have been thrown onto the streets because of an inadequate mental health system.

For many, the only therapy they receive is from groups like mine. It's hard to believe that in the United States, our mentally ill are treated like pariahs, as many spend their lives looking for answers. Some of those suffering from mental illness will realize there is hope and help to see them through their gloomiest days. As I tell in this book, in the early seventies I was so desperate for relief that I came very close to killing myself and my father. If not for guidance from many psychiatrists, psychologists, and family and friends, I wouldn't be in the shape I'm in today.

There are two outcomes I want people to take away from my memoir. First, with hope and empathy from a lot of professional mental health experts and my family and friends, I was able to turn my life around. It was not easy, and it took a lot of years. But now I am content with my life and enjoy every minute of it. That means that if I can conquer bipolar disorder, so can anyone else who is suffering from mental health issues. Believe me. There is good help available, but you must seek it out and stick with it. It will be worth the journey.

The second outcome I hope for is that the so-called *normal* people will discover that those with mental issues are not to be shunned and thought of as inferior. Many people are susceptible to bouts of depression, mania, or other issues but won't admit it. They never get help or take medication because they think it won't help, or they believe they can handle their problems by themselves. Nothing could be further from the truth.

ABOUT THE AUTHOR

Steve Wilson, seventy-three, has spent a lifetime battling bipolar disorder. Despite his roller-coaster ride through the ups and downs of being bipolar, he and his wife, Lenni, have been able to raise their daughters Jami, Cari, and Casi to become inspirational adults. Their granddaughter, Mia, has completed her first year as an elementary school art teacher. Avery, granddaughter two, has just graduated from Ohio State University with honors.

In addition to his family, Wilson has achieved three important milestones. After struggling mightily for many years, he has been able to conquer (for the most part) his battle with bipolar disorder. Since then, he has spent a lot of his time as the facilitator for two mental health support groups in Phoenix, Arizona, working to help those afflicted with mental health problems navigate through life. Finally, he has written this important book that chronicles his life consumed with bipolar disorder, so other sufferers can see that no matter how bad your situation, you can receive the help you need.